OVERCOMING
IMPOSSIBLE

OVERCOMING
IMPOSSIBLE

Learn to Lead, Build a
Team, and Catapult Your
Business to Success

ROBERT IRVINE

WITH MATT TUTHILL

HarperCollins
LEADERSHIP

AN IMPRINT OF HarperCollins

DISCARD

CARLSBAD CA 92011

Published by HarperCollins Leadership, an imprint of HarperCollins Focus LLC.

Book design by Aubrey Khan, Neuwirth & Associates, Inc.
Fork and Knife by Hasanudin from NounProject.com

Any internet addresses, phone numbers, or company or product information printed in this book are offered as a resource and are not intended in any way to be or to imply an endorsement by HarperCollins Leadership, nor does HarperCollins Leadership vouch for the existence, content, or services of these sites, phone numbers, companies, or products beyond the life of this book.

ISBN 978-1-4002-3834-7 (eBook)
ISBN 978-1-4002-3833-0 (HC)

Library of Congress Control Number: 2022944801

Printed in the United States of America
23 24 25 26 27 LSC 10 9 8 7 6 5 4 3 2 1

For anyone who ever looked up at the stars in the night sky, thought of the thing they always wanted most, and whispered, "Someday . . ."

CONTENTS

Introduction   xi

PART 1
Overcoming Impossible in Your Business

ONE   The Number-One Business Killer   3
TWO   Mise en Place   33
THREE   It's Not Their Job to Get It   61
FOUR   Social Media: A Blessing and a Curse   79
FIVE   Is It All about Money?   107

PART 2
Overcoming Impossible in Your Mindset

SIX   Know Your Why   127
SEVEN   Managing Ego   151
EIGHT   Win the Day   171
NINE   Work-Life Balance   189

Acknowledgments   209
Index   213
About the Authors   219

OVERCOMING
IMPOSSIBLE

INTRODUCTION

What I've learned, and what I can teach you

I live on the road.

I have a home near Tampa and it's quite nice. Someday I'm sure I'll spend a lot of time there.

For now, though, my life is lived on a plane, out of a suitcase, and in a new hotel room practically every night. That's the path I chose. Something is always keeping me on the go—filming for one of my shows, visiting the troops at home and abroad, my live tour, or—as is increasingly the case—a business venture of some sort.

I'm not complaining. I love living this way, and if it were up to me, I'd probably do it forever. I find it incredibly stimulating to wake up in a different place almost every day, and nothing makes me feel more vital than meeting new people.

As time has gone on and I've become known as much for my business acumen as my skills in the kitchen, the nature of my interactions with people has slanted in one direction: everyone wants to know what it takes to be successful.

Aspiring entrepreneurs, would-be restaurateurs, and practically every shade of businessperson in between—people stuck somewhere on a corporate ladder they don't want to be on—come up to me and tell me they want something more. And they don't just want more money. Sure, that's part of it, but money isn't all of it or even most of it. Trust me, plenty of these people who feel so terribly trapped in their career make a handsome salary that would be the envy of just about anybody.

Part of the issue is that oftentimes their jobs don't take advantage of their full range of talents. Say they get hired to crunch numbers but management doesn't want to hear their analysis of those numbers or any creative solutions they might bring to the table. In many instances, the finished product they help produce simply doesn't hold any meaning for them. The unifying factor for all these folks is that none of them feel fulfilled by their work. That's not a feeling any of us should brush aside, but so often that's just what we do.

No, I don't like my job, but it pays the bills, so who am I to complain?

Sure, I'd love to change careers or open my own business, but it could get rough. Can I really put the kids through that?

Shouldn't I just be grateful that I have a stable job at all? I know a lot of people who'd kill for what I have.

I'll bet you've said some version of all these things to yourself at some point.

You can couch these statements in the noble sentiment of maintaining perspective and self-awareness, but when you take that framing away, they look an awful lot like excuses, don't they? Don't get me wrong, they're good excuses—even great ones. Shit, you practically have me convinced that something bigger isn't meant for you.

Except there's something about the way these statements are spoken that so often lacks authenticity. The speaker's voice goes up an octave as they explain themselves, and if you read their body language, they usually look a little tight—nature's way of prepping us to go on the defensive.

And why go on the defensive at the notion that the line of work you're in might be the wrong one?

Lots of reasons. For one thing, if you admit that you're in the wrong job, you then might have to admit you've wasted a lot of your time. For another, if you acknowledge that it's time to move on, well, you've now got a ton of work ahead of you, don't you? And won't that disrupt your routine? The cozy little corner of the planet you've carved out for yourself? And even though your job sucks, your boss is cool enough and never gives you a hard time about PTO and occasionally working from home and all the rest?

Isn't that good enough?

I don't know. You tell me.

But be honest when you do, because if I had to guess, the fact that you're reading this at all means you want more out of your life and career.

If you were sitting in front of me, now's the point where you'd probably ask me two questions. At least that's what everyone else does. It's always the same two questions, too. First, they want to know how I made it. Second, they want advice so they can make it, too.

To answer the first part: I could tell you the whole story of how I made it—how I took the leap from cooking on a ship's galley in the British Royal Navy to working in a big fancy American restaurant. How I then made the bigger jump from kitchens to television—to *Dinner: Impossible*, *Restaurant: Impossible*, and a bunch of others. How I then parlayed that into a family of brands and companies that will outlast my time on this Earth.

But I don't know if such a memoir would do you much good. Some of those details might be instructive, but if you're not already on a similar path to the one I was on, a lot of it might look too alien for you to be able to draw the right parallels between my story and yours.

Besides, the world has changed a lot since I launched my career. The way we do business, communicate with one another, and share information has been radically transformed by the internet—to such a degree that the story of me launching my career in the late 1990s and early 2000s has little relevance to today's world.

But I can answer the second part because my path has taught me a lot. About the evergreen obstacles you're bound to face on your journey. About the types of people you'll meet—the ones you need to surround yourself with and the ones you need to avoid. About the cyclical nature of marketplaces, how to manage egos, how to pitch and sell, and, most importantly, how to deal with failure. Because the truth is I've been kicked around and taken quite a few losses—or, to borrow some sports terminology, taken a few L's. But there is no better teacher than failure. From the ashes of those L's, I've built a career I'm quite proud of—something that's bigger and more satisfying than I ever dreamed was possible.

While there's no way to the top without taking a few L's of your own, it's my hope that with this book in your hands, you won't have to take quite as many as I did. And when you do take an L, you'll be armed with the tools you need to find the lesson in the experience, and you'll emerge stronger and better prepared as a result. None of this is going to be easy. Things that are worth it never are.

But one thing that I learned by taking all those L's is that it only takes a single W to wipe them all off the board. That has always been true and it always will be. When the blood, sweat, and tears are converted into the life and career you've always wanted, all the hardship, well, it won't feel like a distant memory. It will feel like something even better. Like it all had meaning. Like it all led you to the place you were destined to be.

The job that you were too big for, the people who stood in your way and told you that you weren't good enough to move on, your first futile attempts at building something of your very own . . . you'll be thankful for all of it. Because all those bitter defeats make the taste of victory that much sweeter.

But allow me to reiterate: building your own successful brand and business is a Herculean effort. And there is no single book that can teach you how to do everything perfectly and clear all obstacles before you begin. No difficult endeavor works that way—certainly not business. But by the end of this book, you will know the obstacles to look for, how to approach, avoid, or overcome them, and how to equip yourself and your team with a winning mindset that will see you to the promised land, whatever that may look like for you.

Since the road is paved with innumerable difficulties, persistence is a prerequisite that I'm afraid you can't begin your journey without. Persistence, I've learned, is just another word for faith, and I'm asking you to put that faith in yourself, no matter how difficult things get.

After all, people build great things every day. So look in the mirror and ask, *Why not me? Why not now?* and then attack each day with a mindset that one way or another, you're going to get there. You'll be tempted to ask if you're ready for all that's to come. Don't do that, because no one's ever ready. Not really. You *get* ready by doing the work and persisting.

Along the way, you just need to remind yourself of the words I live by: *nothing is impossible.*

Now, let's get to work.

PART 1

Overcoming Impossible in Your Business

ONE

The Number-One Business Killer

Micromanaging is the death knell of any type of business. Here's what you need to do instead.

Joe Willy's Fish Shack

Joe White didn't know how to let go. He had built his seafood restaurant in Fishkill, New York, from scratch. From the menu items to the décor in the dining room, Joe Willy's Fish Shack wasn't so much a restaurant as it was a physical manifestation of the passions of one man. As with so many restaurants, things were great until one day they just weren't. Once it was no longer the new ticket in town, the restaurant struggled as interest waned. Revenue dropped, and in the scramble to find a solution, the man behind the whole thing seemed to abandon the curiosity and passion that had fueled him to open the restaurant in the first place.

By the time I visited Joe Willy's in early 2013, the restaurant wasn't the only thing in disrepair; Joe's marriage to his wife, Dena, had hit the skids, too. As Dena was clocking long hours in the restaurant alongside her husband (on top of working shifts as a server in *another* restaurant to make ends meet), he began to see her less as his wife and partner, and more as another employee.

To make matters worse, Joe was not a good boss. He worked incredibly hard and cared deeply about the restaurant, but he wasn't an effective leader. He micromanaged every aspect of the day-to-day operations. In his head, he was doing it because he felt he had no other choice. After all, he had been the one to design and build every aspect of the place, so who knew it better than him? Who better to fix it? But even though a sense of responsibility was guiding his actions, he was tearing his staff apart. Every time he stepped in to take over a task or refused to delegate, he was in effect telling his employees, "I don't trust you."

Some of the problems his restaurant faced were unique to his situation (for one thing, the restaurant was set much too far back from the road, making foot traffic nonexistent), but the really big ones that were crippling his operations were common to small businesses everywhere. Besides a refusal to delegate so that he could step back and get a better view of the big picture, he was stubborn to a fault.

At one point during the renovation—and during one of the rare moments when the cameras happened to be off—I turned to Joe and told him just that.

"You're too stubborn, man!" I said. "You're surrounded by great people but you can't even see it because you won't let them do anything!"

Abashed, he turned red for a second, but remained defiant. "You know," he said, "I bet you were pretty stubborn when you were starting out, too."

"Yes," I replied, "but the difference is, I'm not broke!"

In short, he had stopped learning, and any business led by someone who reaches a place where they can't be taught is as good as dead.

Spoiler alert: the restaurant, now named Joe Willy's Seafood House, is thriving today. As of June 2022, more than nine years after my first visit, revenue is way up. They've moved into a better location, too, and it's much easier for townsfolk to see it every day and say, "Hey, I wanna try that." The swift kick in the ass I gave Joe helped, obviously. The renovations and promotion on national TV, of course, didn't hurt, either. But every place featured on *Restaurant: Impossible* gets the benefit of these things. Long-term success requires more. It requires the owner to make a real internal change, and not everyone can do it. Joe, to his credit, made significant changes and stuck with them.

For starters, he stopped treating his wife like an employee, which lifted a tension that was palpable enough for customers to feel. More importantly, he learned how to delegate. He stopped micromanaging his staff, and, in the ultimate show of faith, turned over head chef duties to his son. These changes weren't just key from a personal development standpoint, but hugely important in terms of the bottom line. They allowed for new creative strokes of genius that only a diversity of viewpoints could provide—and they made Joe Willy's a restaurant that gave customers a high-quality experience on a more consistent basis.

Joe learned that leadership means empowering others and ultimately letting go. The truth is: no matter how good you are and how hard you work, you'll always get more done as a team than you ever could by yourself. It's a hard lesson for a control freak to learn. I should know; you're listening to the guy who planned every aspect of his own wedding. And I'm very particular about how my businesses work, especially in the kitchen. But in recent years, my businesses have grown exponentially in direct proportion to what I was able to let go of and let others handle. Napoleon Hill wrote that you will always be paid more for "what you can induce others to do" than what you can do on your own. I've found this maxim to be absolutely true.

This translates into working smarter, not harder. It means valuing the macro view as much as the micro view. It means trusting your people and loving them for their efforts, even when that effort doesn't necessarily translate into its intended result.

I built my businesses—Robert Irvine Foods, FitCrunch, my restaurants, and more—by becoming a better leader and setting the example that I wanted others to follow, not by trying to do it all by myself. I take it as an article of faith that if you are smart about what you're trying to accomplish and can set a standard of excellence for others to emulate, then your business, and your life, can be enriched beyond your wildest dreams.

I've seen so many people accomplish more than what they ever felt was possible that I've wiped the word "impossible" from my everyday vocabulary. The magic of this life is that we get to decide what is possible. With a strong enough belief and a work ethic to match, I say anything is possible.

Joe White knows how true that is, and he's got a thriving restaurant to prove it.

What will you have?

LEADERSHIP AND THE VALUE OF EMPOWERING OTHERS

The central tenet of my leadership style is trust

I trust my employees to get their work done to a high standard and in a timely fashion. I trust that in all their day-to-day operations, they recognize that by representing my companies, they, in essence, serve as my emissaries to the world. They need to treat people as I would, knowing that everything they do—positive or negative—reflects upon me. If we're being totally honest about the reality of the social media age, each one of my employees is a single bad day in a grocery store away from causing immeasurable damage to the bottom line. That's life when everyone's got a video camera in their pocket.

For the employees with purchasing power, I trust them to respect that responsibility and spend company money as if it were their own. Most importantly, I trust that they are as invested in the future of these companies as I am, because at the end of the day, whether we reach our full potential largely depends upon them.

I've had a lot of good ideas in my time as a business leader. But if the company's success were dependent on me providing every idea, we'd be sunk. And so I invest in this final, most vital, area of trust: I trust that my employees will call upon all their creative faculties and passions and bring them to the table every day.

How am I able to do this?

As with kitchen prep work—where all the tedious stuff is done before the busy dinner service so you're not scrambling—by the time I've committed to hiring someone, I've already used every tool at my disposal to determine whether they are the right fit for the job. When they sign on, they experience a relatively brief onboarding where they get to know everyone and how we do things, and then they're off and running, masters of whatever domain they've been hired to rule over. I don't spend one minute looking over their shoulders. I micromanage nothing.

So many business owners and managers are afraid to afford this kind of trust to their employees, and I get it. It's not easy to give up control, especially when you're used to having your fingers on everything. But if you've made the right hires—and adequately assessed their character—then I can assure you this is the best route to take.

In high-character people, being trusted completely intensifies work ethic and a desire to contribute to the company rather than—as the worries go—diminish it. If I'm only checking in with someone once every couple of days—or even weeks—as shooting schedules sometimes dictate, then they're eager to be able to deliver, or show me how much progress they've made with a project, when I do check in.

Conversely, micromanaging these same types of people has a dispiriting effect that diminishes returns. And it makes sense. If you're a trustworthy, hardworking person who is regularly treated as if you're not trustworthy or hardworking by way of excessive monitoring or questioning, you would rightly be offended. Or, if you weren't outright offended, you might just get that sneaking feeling that this job isn't the right fit. After all, your bosses don't see you for who you are, so are they really worthy of your greatest effort? Your best ideas? The full force of your passion and ambition?

Finding high-character people, of course, is the linchpin in exhibiting this type of trust and harnessing the potential it unlocks. I emphasize this fact because I haven't always made the right hires. Sometimes I saw great talent and work ethic and punctuality but missed something else, some other flaw. In a few instances, I missed an employee's desire to just be part of the after-party and cash in on the ancillary benefits of being associated with a hit TV show. In others, it took some time to reveal that a person wasn't as intrinsically motivated as they needed to be when entrusted with total freedom in a position of authority.

I had to fire these employees—and it felt horrible to do so—but I checked the impulse to label these episodes as failures. Each bad hire—and thankfully there have only been a few—was a revelation for me. These situations taught me to dig deeper and look harder at who the whole person is. They also taught me that the high-wire act of the entrepreneurial life simply isn't for everyone. It can decimate highly talented people who might flourish in a conventional setting. It also reaffirmed that the real keepers—the employees in my inner circle who thrive on the high-risk, high-reward path that I've chosen for our companies—deserve to be richly rewarded. That goes for compensation, recognition, and freedom. It's a circular affirmation of the fact that trust is still the best policy.

Setting Expectations for Employees

Clearly articulate what you need from your people— and be ready to lead by example

I never ask any of my employees to do anything that I wouldn't do myself. If you've ever seen one episode of *Restaurant: Impossible*, you know I've got nothing against rolling up my sleeves (just kidding, I never wear long sleeves) and slinging a mop, cleaning grease traps, or knocking down walls with my trusty sledgehammer. To me, this is a basic aspect of leading by example. And yet, so many business owners don't get it. They think that because they already had to do the dirty jobs when they were coming up, those days are behind them. Again, I get it. When times are good and everything is running smoothly, they're right. But the moment your employees begin to struggle under a massive workload or a crushing deadline, the best thing you can do is jump into the fray and help! You know how to do all the stuff they're trying to do! Don't delegate. Don't manage. Just do. They don't need a manager right now—they need an extra set of hands. If you're too stubborn or proud to offer them that, you need to prepare for the consequences, which will be visited upon your bottom line.

Pitching in on menial tasks has the ancillary effect of intensifying team bonding and allowing your employees to witness another side of you they'd otherwise never have a chance to see. You won't lower your perceived stature; you'll enhance it, command more respect, and build trust. Employees won't have a moment to think of a tough or dirty job as punishment or a lack of respect for their ability. Instead of thinking "Ah, shit, he's making us do *this* again," they'll simply hop to and get it done because they've seen you do just that.

Thinking you're "too good" for the little tasks isn't limited to CEOs of big companies. There are folks who own tiny, hole-in-the-wall diners in the middle of nowhere who don't get it. While filming one episode of *Restaurant: Impossible,* I popped into the kitchen to find the chef standing around, waiting for orders—with no one in the restaurant—while a stack of dirty dishes sat in a pile.

I was genuinely confused and assumed I had missed something.

"Why are those dishes just sitting there?" I asked.

"Dishwasher isn't in yet," he told me.

"OK. So why don't you do them?" I pressed.

"I'm a chef. I don't do dishes."

I was incensed. Here was a guy who was willing to let filth accumulate around him because he deemed the task of cleaning it up too small for him. I made my point, emphatically, that—especially in small operations—everyone needs to be willing to pitch in with everything when the need arises. He eventually got it. But the lesson here is to hire people who are helpful to begin with—not people you'll have to cajole into doing the right thing.

There are lots of ways of divining how someone will behave when the shit hits the fan. Hiring someone on a trial basis or using a probation period is one way, but I prefer not to do this. Owing to what I wrote earlier in this section about trust, a probation or trial period explicitly says, "I don't trust you yet." Alternatively, spend time with that person outside of the interview or work situation if possible. A few days after the initial interview, you can ask them to grab a coffee to catch up. Just have a conversation and find out what makes them tick. Do they volunteer at their local church or community center in their spare time? Do they donate to charity? Coach a kids' team? Tutor? Then maybe in the course of conversation you can slyly toss in a hypothetical about what they'd do in a sticky situation that has actually come up in your business. What's your version of the dirty pile of dishes?

Make a comprehensive list of everything one of your employees must do during the course of the day for your business to be successful. What are you missing? What are you taking for granted? What expectations do your current employees meet without you having to explicitly express them? If you have great employees already and you're looking to expand, be aware that you might have just been lucky to this point in your hiring. Especially if you're working with a small handful of ground-level employees who understood your goals from the outset. If you're past those first few rocky months or year or two, congrats! Let me be the one to remind you that the real peril begins now: at the moment your confidence grows and you start making big decisions at a more rapid pace.

Slow down. Look around you and think hard about what's working. Realize that putting together a team is like putting together a puzzle. Make sure all the pieces are going to fit; jamming one in can damage the pieces and ruin the picture. And make sure they're the type of person who will mesh well with your leadership style. If your gut makes you feel unsure, listen to it. Ask every question you can to assuage the concern. If a potential hire is put off by how thorough you want to be, then that's a clear indication they're probably not right for the job.

Deraney's Two City Tavern

That cook who wouldn't do dishes had *nothing* on Christopher Deraney.

Don't get me wrong. Christopher had a big heart. The grandson of Joe and Mable Deraney—local legends who ran their namesake department store in Barnesville, Georgia, for the better part of a century—Christopher was eager to keep the Deraney name alive in Barnesville, and opened Deraney's Two City Tavern as a way of honoring his grandparents' memory and paying homage to their legacy.

Naturally, a few problems cropped up. For starters, Christopher didn't know anything about running a restaurant. Worse, it didn't appear that Christopher had inherited his grandparents' work ethic.

The restaurant was $190,000 in the red by the time I arrived, and the loans keeping it afloat were leveraged against Grandma's house and the old department store. If this thing went under, it wasn't just the end of an ill-advised adventure into the restaurant industry, but the end of the legacy he was fighting to protect.

This episode continued a recent trend on the show where the restaurant's problems weren't really technical or culinary—though the menu and dining room of course needed some sprucing up—but interpersonal. Christopher's penchant for showing up late, micromanaging a few small tasks, then ducking out before the thankless tasks of cleanup and closing even began rubbed staff the wrong way. The knock-on effect was significant.

"The side work doesn't get done because he's eager to get people off the clock," one staffer said, explaining that it was then even harder to open up the next day. Christopher not only saw himself as too big for the little things, but actively stopped his staff—who wanted to do this stuff!—from getting them done. From his perspective, he was the money man and the brains behind the operation, and those folks aren't *really* beholden to the strictures of punctuality, are they? Oh boy . . .

During the course of the show, he realized he had an entitlement problem, at last admitting that he hadn't lived up to the Deraney name and what it was supposed to mean. The name would only be associated with people's positive memories of Christopher's grandparents and their store for so long. If he kept going along the same path he was headed, that name would mean something totally different.

In fact, it was already moving in that direction. In the words of the customers—who wouldn't speak on camera because they feared offending him directly—they saw Christopher as pretentious and abrasive, with one commenter pointing out that despite the restaurant's considerable debts, Christopher still found a way to throw lavish parties, further alienating himself from the townsfolk.

In a tearful mea culpa, Christopher vowed to his staff that he would change and lead from the front. "I promise you this," Christopher said, "when there is slack, I will pull it. When the next storm comes, I will lead the charge facing it head on. And when one of you is in need, I will do all that I can to help you because you all have stopped at nothing to do that for me. Now it is my turn and my privilege to do the same for you. I love you all so very much."

No one on the staff rejected the apology or saw it as a hollow promise. They knew Christopher well and knew he wasn't a bad guy; he just didn't have the perspective to see himself honestly or fully appreciate the effect his actions had on the rest of the staff.

With those scales removed from his eyes, business jumped, and as of this writing, Deraney's remains on a good path. If Christopher slips backward into his old ways, he can be sure sales will eventually follow. If he can find joy in his work—and appreciate work in a worthy task as its own reward—then he and his staff can rest easy.

Invest in Your People and They Will Invest in You

How meaningful connection with employees will pay you back a thousandfold

By the time a business becomes a big corporation, it's unreasonable to think new hires will automatically become invested in the company's mission statement or corporate responsibility initiatives. At a certain point, size can be a hindrance that prevents most employees from forming a bond with or loyalty to the company name.

God willing, that's a problem you'll have one day, and what a luxurious problem it will be! For now, however, you don't have to worry about this one, and you've got the benefit of being able to spend some time to understand the personalities who work under you and figure out what motivates them.

It may very well be that what motivates your employees is totally unrelated to the business you're in and there's no way to encourage them to express their creativity and pursue those passions through their work for you. But it's perfectly reasonable that you show an interest in what interests them.

Imagine if you had the benefit of going to work in a place where your boss regularly asked you about how your . . . classic car restoration, sci-fi short story, flower garden, home brewing project, et cetera, was coming along. It would be nice to be around someone who cares about what you care about, wouldn't it? Or at least someone who recognizes that these things are important to you?

Then, over time, wouldn't you become more invested in seeing your boss realize their dreams and goals?

And that's where your employees absolutely can help you because they already work for you and are thus part of the machinery whose function is to realize your goals.

This is simple human bonding. Through evolution, we're hardwired to care about people who care about us. It's how we build community and reach further as a society.

My businesses are well diversified and I'm fortunate to have found employees who are intrinsically motivated to do the work they've been hired to do. To enhance my bonds with my people, I'm able to give them ownership of various corners of Robert Irvine Enterprises and see them apply that passion and creativity in ways I never would have imagined and thus strengthen the company in unique ways only those particular people could.

But I'm not naïve, either. I know that hiring such high-powered individuals means some of them have aspirations beyond working for me and eventually want ownership over their own thing. If you're doing it right, you're bound to run into the same issue. In that case, I make sure that their continued employment with me is worth their while—not just in terms of their compensation but in terms of the mentorship I can offer. If my companies are places where they can learn and grow and make a living at the same time, that's a recipe for even higher engagement. When the environment is so stimulating and enriching that they're excited to go to work each day, that's going to pay off in spades.

Some of them will, of course, eventually outgrow their roles and leave at a certain point. This is OK! In my experience, "losing" good people may hurt in the short term, but pays off as those folks sing your praises within the industry and serve as de facto recruiters for your company. After all, you did right by them, so they'll want to do right by you.

If you're not naturally possessed of expert people-reading skills, fear not. Straight-up asking your employees what excites them most in life is a perfectly valid approach. Asking how you can help them develop along their professional path is also smart. It's not always apparent even if you are good at reading people. Remember that not everyone is getting the interest or validation they crave at home. Spouses tend to get wrapped up in their own professional pursuits, and if they've got kids, it can become rare for them to check in on each other. Sad but true. If your relationship with your employees can replace the interest and validation that they're not getting from traditional sources, then you've now occupied a coveted place in their minds. Loyalty and trust will follow—not to mention the best work they're capable of.

Key to getting the most out of your employees is forging a real connection with them. None of the above works if you view it as some Jedi mind trick where feigned interest unlocks productivity.

I'd like to think that if you ran into any of my employees on the street and asked them what it's like to work for me, they'd tell you that we have fun, that we work hard and play just as hard, and that Team Irvine is more like a family than a collection of colleagues. Yeah, lots of companies say that, I know. Whatever. Like I said, talk to my employees. We care about each other and are invested in each other's lives. We pick each other up when we suffer failure and loss, and are there to celebrate one another's victories. And we have *a lot* of fun—when the day's work is done, of course.

I like to think this feeling starts at the top. I've always striven to build a creative and supportive work environment, but it's come to fruition for me because I hired good people. Not just talented and hardworking, but good people in a more general sense. People who are present, authentic, caring, and generous. In short: *real*. I don't have an entourage; I have my people! I'd rather go to happy hour with my team than anyone else. The fact that we get to build something together is a terrific bonus.

Life is short. And because of the way we center work in our society, you wind up spending more time with your coworkers than you do with your actual family. You can debate the pros and cons of that all you'd like, but that's a bigger issue for a different kind of book. All I'm saying is that if this dynamic happens to be the case right now, the least I can do as a business leader is create the best environment possible. Time at work away from your real family shouldn't have to feel like a major sacrifice, and for the most part, I think I've achieved that.

ACCOUNTABILITY

*You can't own a business without
owning your mistakes*

From the biggest companies to the smallest, the healthiest businesses are the ones that operate in a culture of accountability. For everyone in the company, this means acknowledging any screw-ups, shortcomings, or oversights—owning what goes wrong as readily as what goes right.

When I point out a screw-up in my company, I don't want an apology. In fact, spending a lot of time on an apology is one of the surest ways to push me from concerned to fully annoyed. I get it. It's natural to say you're sorry if you screwed up. Fine. Say it once, then move on. The next words out of your mouth should be solutions. My life and my companies thrive on forward momentum. Agonizing over errors and indulging in self-flagellation is the death of that momentum.

Here's an example: when we were building Fresh Kitchen by Robert Irvine—my restaurant inside the Pentagon that serves the men and women who work at the Department of Defense—it was always the intention that one of the main attractions was going to be our pizza oven. There are a lot of people who work there who just don't have the time to sit for a meal and need to be able to grab something quickly as they pass by. That original intention, which seemed so simple on paper, hit a number of serious and increasingly costly setbacks, from a shockingly complicated equipment delivery process because of where the restaurant was located within the building, to the fact that the oven was so heavy that the floor where it would be situated needed to be reinforced.

With every step of the process, more money kept flying out the window for something that, again, should have been relatively simple and affordable for a project of this nature. Should these obstacles have been identified by folks on the ground before we began the project? Sure. Did it help to do a postmortem on the situation afterward to ensure we never ran into problems like these again? Yes. But there's a big difference between doing that—which I would categorize as accountability—and poring over the details with the intention of knocking subordinates down a peg. The former allows for learning and growth. The latter—disciplining them like children—instills fear and hesitation and doesn't give you better, more competent employees; it gives you people who play it safe. They won't want to swing for the fences anymore; they'll want to narrow their focus to the point where they know they can't make any mistakes.

I'm happy to say that everyone learned a lot from the experience. For my part, it reminded me of how difficult and complicated all aspects of building a new restaurant can be, and to be grateful when things turn out to be relatively straightforward.

As your company grows and takes on more projects, there will be more instances where you as the leader will only see the finished product, and not all the blood, sweat, and tears that went into getting it ready. When your employees deliver a winner, be free and generous with praise. It's not just important for morale; it's key that you treat both sides of accountability—the good as well as the bad—with the same amount of attention.

You can learn a lot about potential hires by asking them about projects—both the successes and the disasters—at their previous companies. Try some variation of this: *I saw you guys launched that new artisanal chewing gum six months ago. Who* *knew people would pay $14 for a pack?! Congrats!* Then take note of how much credit the person claims for themselves, and how much they defer to their team members. Later on, you can ask about the launch of their gas-powered toddler tricycle and the bevy of lawsuits they're now facing. There's always plenty of blame to go around in failure, so it's OK if the story begins with the misguided actions of other coworkers, but note how much blame your candidate takes for themself. Their grace, or lack thereof, can tell you a lot about them and how they'll behave in similar situations going forward.

ACCOUNTABILITY
RESTAURANT: IMPOSSIBLE CASE STUDY

Café No Fur

If you're a bit confused the first time you come across the words "Café No Fur," I'm with you. I was baffled when I arrived in Las Vegas to help this struggling fast-food restaurant, and its name—an apparent reference to its vegan cuisine—was just the beginning. It was a filthy, depressing little place with dirty pink paint and bad art that more closely resembled an abandoned nail salon than a restaurant. The dining room—with exposed vents and wiring—wasn't up to code, and the menu was just as off-putting. You'd think an all-vegan restaurant would offer, I dunno, some fresh vegetables, maybe? Ha. Café No Fur wasn't that kind of place—all frozen junk and reconstituted bits of imitation chicken and beef. The head chef didn't cook. She rehydrated highly processed science fair projects and chucked them in the microwave.

Sounds atrocious—and it was—but I'll be honest; in the annals of *Restaurant: Impossible*, it's not anywhere near the worst I've seen. Yet it was a uniquely galling experience to be there and witness this mess. Here was a place over $80,000 in the hole, and when I pointed this out to owner Kevin Chan and his co-owner Yhessa Gonzales, I was met with excuse after excuse.

In the dozens of one-star reviews, customers complained not just about absurd wait times, but a waitstaff that didn't even check in with them throughout the course of their meal. Yhessa, ostensibly in charge of the front of the house, defiantly told me she was "doing her best" and that she was "only twenty-four."

Meanwhile, Kevin refused to lead. In an effort to ensure his employees liked their place of work, he resorted to an extreme style of laid-back management: no rules and no systems. Well, that explained the inches of dust in the corners, anyway. As part of the do-what-you-want atmosphere, Yhessa at least got to do what she did best: pose for Instagram pictures with the food.

Yes, I know social media is important, and I'll get to that later, but this situation sent me into a tizzy. "Posting pictures on social media isn't running a business!" I yelled.

A lot needed to happen in two days, and we got a lot done. Working alone, with Tom Bury out on paternity leave, designer Lynn Kegan pulled off a beautiful and fitting redesign, and I taught Kevin and his kitchen staff how amazing vegan food can be when it's made with a bit of love. And since portobello mushrooms, black beans, and tofu are a hell of a lot cheaper than steak and lobster, the profit margins ought to turn Café No Fur into a gold mine.

Affecting the type of attitude shift I needed from Kevin and Yhessa, on the other hand, wasn't easy. It was deeply uncomfortable for everyone. It's not my trademark to start yelling to create a scene for the cameras; there are plenty of episodes where I'm concerned, but if I'm not really angry or feel a need to yell, I don't do it. Well, I yelled a lot in this one because I was genuinely pissed. The lack of accountability for so many different flavors of failure was beyond exasperating.

After two straight days of my drawing a direct line between the lack of accountability and the red ink on the balance sheet, it finally dawned on them. When the buck doesn't stop anywhere, the customers are the ones who suffer. When the employees are empowered to take ownership and are led by a confident hand, then you've got a magical place to work. Employees don't really want an environment with no rules; they want to be engaged in a worthy cause and feel proud of what they create.

Today, in Kevin's words, Café No Fur "sells an experience, not just food."

Before I left, he added, "You showed me things I didn't even think were possible."

I had to smile. And you can probably guess what I told him next.

THE VALUE OF
EMOTIONAL INTELLIGENCE

*How deftly managing interpersonal
relationships can strengthen your business*

When evaluating potential partners and employees, I'm always looking for emotional intelligence. In all my initial interactions with people, I observe carefully and ask questions. Does this person lack self-awareness? Can they control their own egotistical desire to dominate a conversation and make it all about them?

It's not enough to recruit the smartest or most talented people for the job. In addition to having mastered the requisite skills, I need to know if you can read a situation. Can you read people? Can you empathize with them? Can you walk into a room with one plan and then drop it when you get a sense that your plan, for whatever reason, isn't going to work with these particular people at this particular time?

Here are three short stories that will demonstrate exactly what I'm talking about. In these stories, you're going to learn all about emotional intelligence from people I will call Employees A, B, and C.

First, Employee A. This was a guy I once partnered with on a few projects, and he was, in almost all ways, a joy to be around. He was boisterous, positive, and exciting. On top of being knowledgeable and accomplished in his field and possessing special expertise that I didn't have, he had a way of finding people who were plagued by self-doubt and, within minutes, convincing them that they were an invincible warrior capable of magnificent deeds. He could mold people and imbue them with confidence at blinding speed. I was certain I wanted to be in this person's orbit forever and that he would become integral to the future of the company.

But his emotional intelligence—as advanced as it was in one area—was incomplete. Because as good as he was at building people up, he was also mystifyingly oblivious when it came time to read a room. To wit, we were traveling with the USO, visiting troops in remote areas of the Middle East who hadn't seen their spouses or children in months—and were in constant danger of perhaps never seeing them again—and to my unending shock, this guy couldn't stop talking about himself. His big career feats. His celebrity friends. His business plans. And on and on, all in front of bedraggled and overworked soldiers who at that moment, more than anything, needed to be entertained, to lie down, and to temporarily forget their considerable burdens.

It was gut wrenching to part ways with Employee A—the skills that he did possess are damn near impossible to replicate—but what else was I supposed to do? I wasn't asking him to be a mind-reader. But if your ego or some other facet of your personality prevents you from making such a fundamentally easy judgment call to shut up about yourself for two seconds, you're no longer an asset. You're a liability.

The trouble with emotional intelligence is that, at least as far as my experience has been concerned, it's unteachable. You either have it or you don't. You can get by with a little. It's better if you have a lot. If you've got none, you're shit outta luck in most fields. Steer clear of people who weren't blessed with even a modicum of emotional intelligence. Their lack of tact in a key situation, be it an off-color joke during a negotiation or a bungled interaction with a customer or client, could cause a lot of headaches and cost you a lot of money.

Now let's have a look at what the opposite can get you in the case of Employee B.

Employee B lacked any skills that you would call specialized. But I loved him because he worked his ass off and always got the job done. While I was certain the clerical work he did could be quickly replaced at need with a want ad, I was less certain that his potential replacement would possess the same high level of emotional intelligence. Because this employee knew how to read the room, and he always knew how to read me. He was quick with a joke, but he never cracked one at the wrong time. He was laid-back but could respond immediately to alleviate a tense room with just the right suggestion. As if by magic, every time I was agitated, there he was with a cup of Earl Grey, the perfect balm to soothe any Englishman's nerves.

In short, he simply "got it," fitting in perfectly with the company culture and finding creative ways to make himself useful at just the right moments. He also wanted to learn, could take feedback—positive and negative—and build off it. Someone like that? I don't care that he didn't hold any unique certifications or outwardly appeared to be just another worker bee. After a few months of having him around, he went from easily replaceable to indispensable. That's quite a leap to make, but he did it.

Now, before you go and decide that your own secretary who's always there with an answer or a coffee is a unicorn who can't be replaced, you need to do a little digging. Specifically, find out how this person treats their peers, and even more importantly, how they treat their subordinates.

To illustrate the importance of this point, I'm going to introduce you to the third employee of mine from many years ago, whom we shall call Employee C.

Employee C filled me with confidence. He had specialized skills like Employee A and the emotional intelligence of Employee B. He was laser-focused on delivering crisp, clean work ahead of deadlines. In terms of reading me and the room, there were few who were better. He was supportive of other people's ideas, offered creative solutions of his own, and seemed to have no ego once I made a final decision. Never mind cups of tea, this guy was in my face first thing every morning with a pep in his step, a smile on his face, and the same question every time: "How can I help you today?" And somehow it wasn't rote or phony. When he asked it, you believed it, because whatever my answer was, he found a way to help.

There's only one way for a guy like that to go, right? Up! So I put him in charge of a big project. I sent him ahead of me by a few days to an event where I was set to give a speech, do a cooking demo, and host a meet-and-greet. I do a lot of these around the country for various organizations and companies, and laying all the prep work at the feet of Justin Leonard, my COO, can be a recipe for burnout, so I saw a win-win. Employee C went ahead, and I had enough faith in him that I didn't check in. I just arrived on the day to do my thing.

As far as I could tell, Employee C had knocked it out of the park. Everything went as smoothly as I had hoped. He had delivered in a way that had me eyeing a much bigger role for him within the company.

Then, as I'm wrapping up, the rep for the company for whom I'd just made the appearance came and found me as I was getting in the car to go back to the airport.

"Thanks again for coming, Robert!" she said.

"Yeah, no problem," I replied, but already I was suspicious. We had just done this a few minutes earlier with her whole team. I'm not one for long goodbyes and I didn't think there was much to be sentimental over. So, I added, "Can't wait to come back and do it again."

She took the opening and said, "Yes! Can't wait for that . . . Will Justin be back next time?"

"Um, maybe . . . Did everything go OK with [Employee C]?"

"Oh, you know, he was extremely thorough and detail-oriented. Really a great event organizer . . . Look, I don't want to get anyone in trouble, it's just not my style, but . . ."

She was having a hard time getting it out, so I made it clear she was free to speak her mind.

"Look, if he did something wrong, I need to know."

"That's just the thing!" she replied. "I'd want you to tell me if anything were wrong on your end, too. You know, both of us feel responsible for our people. When they do something right, when they do something wrong . . . or if someone mistreated them. And I just had a lot of concerns brought to my attention this weekend. A lot of the waitstaff and production crew, they said [Employee C] really talked down to them. That anytime he asked for anything, he was unpleasant . . . demanding . . . and, well, more than a bit derisive."

The words hung there in the breeze for a moment. I couldn't believe what I was hearing.

"I am *so* sorry to bring this to your attention!" she continued. "I never want to get anyone in trouble, I just . . . had to speak up for my people."

"Please," I told her. "I'm glad you told me. I'm shocked. I'm sorry. And I can promise you it will never happen again."

We left it at that, but the whole ride back to the airport, I was stewing. Still in stunned disbelief, I felt betrayed. The good vibes of a mission successfully accomplished as I jaunted off to my next location were a distant memory. Now all I had was a pit in my stomach and a burning desire to call up Employee C, give him a piece of my mind, and dismiss him on the spot.

Where had this ego come from? How could he be so careless? And why was he so confident I'd never find out?

I took my phone out and my thumb hovered over his name for a second. But I hesitated.

Never mind what he had done wrong. What had I missed? And how did I miss it so badly? This was a crisis, no doubt, but I've long understood that you can't let any crises go to waste. Learn from them and they can make you better. Fail to learn from them and they'll haunt you long after the immediate danger has passed by showing up again and again.

So I scrolled past his name and instead placed a call to the home office in Tampa. The receptionist picked up.

"Robert! What can I do for you?" she asked.

"Actually, you're just the person I needed to speak to," I said. "You've been around [Employee C] for a while now. Has he ever been . . . a jerk to you? Talked down to you? Anything like that?"

There was silence on the line for a long beat, then . . . "Actually, I'm glad you asked."

She went on to detail almost verbatim the kind of behavior I had just heard from the company rep at the event. I called another entry-level employee. Same story. And then one more call to another employee for good measure. Same story again.

My head was spinning. It felt like a fog had descended on my brain. When your life is as busy as mine and your livelihood thrives on a bias toward action, one of the toughest things to deal with is uncertainty. It's especially tough when you're suddenly plagued by doubts about something you had been dead certain about.

I still felt the urge to call Employee C and give him a loud and decisive farewell, but I had one more call to make. I dialed Justin. I told him everything that had just happened, from the chat with the company rep to the conversations with Employee C's subordinates.

Justin was as blindsided as I had been. As I hung up with him, I finally had clarity. Employee C was a kiss-up-and-kick-down type. These folks are masters at making themselves indispensable to authority figures (in this case, me and Justin), but anyone below them in the pecking order is the proverbial ninety-pound weakling on the beach, and they're all too happy to kick sand in their faces. My wife, Gail, saw a lot of it in the world of professional wrestling, a unique place where on-screen talent like Gail occupy a middle tier, with all-powerful executives at the top and production folks and road crew on the bottom. Gail lost count of how many wrestlers would kiss the boss's ass all day long for a prime spot on the show and in the next breath turn around and act like an absolute monster to the support staff.

As it dawned on me that this was indeed the type of person that Employee C had always been, I finally realized why I missed it: I had not spent enough time communicating with the lowest-level employees. If I had—and made it clear to them that they can be honest with me—I might have seen the truth about Employee C a whole lot sooner and gotten rid of him before he did any reputational damage to my company.

When you're the boss, it's incredibly difficult to spot the ones who kiss up and kick down. The greatest skill possessed by people who kiss up and kick down is usually an uncanny ability to hide their behavior and motives from their superiors, who only ever see their best side. And since they're so good at hiding their behavior, you're often clueless until it's too late—you've handed them a management position and they're making life hell for their subordinates. My employees—god bless 'em—saw how much I liked working with Employee C and saw how useful he was, so they didn't want to flag the issues they had with him.

They felt that as long as the boss was happy, they should just smile and carry on.

In the wake of the Employee C disaster, I've changed my own behavior; namely, I speak as often as I can with everyone from the ground up. Moreover, I've made it explicitly clear to everyone that they're not doing me any favors by not raising an issue just because they don't want to ruin my day. It took someone outside of our company to flag and neutralize a serious issue—and I'm eternally grateful that she did—but it never should have come to that.

No matter the size of your company, never forget that being the boss automatically shields you from certain things. Not only do your people want to make you happy, but they also don't want to snitch. It's been stigmatized—appropriately or not—because no adult ever wants to be seen as unable to handle their own problems. Each one of the employees who Employee C had dumped on shrugged and said, "Damn. That stinks, but I don't want to bother Robert." It's the most natural reaction in the world, and it will happen to you, too, unless you take definitive action to make sure that it doesn't.

It's not enough to simply have an open-door policy. Reach down and have real conversations with people. Find out their concerns and push them a bit if you have to, because they'll probably be reticent to disclose them. Further impress upon them that it isn't snitching if you're saving the company from real reputational harm. If one of my managers is mistreating them, they can be certain that the behavior extends beyond our doors. If left unchecked, it could create an existential crisis for the company.

Last and most importantly, your people bust their ass for you. As a baseline starting point for their efforts, they deserve a work environment free from any form of harassment or humiliation. If you institute a zero-tolerance policy when it comes to protecting your most vulnerable people, you send a loud and clear message that titles don't make one person more important than another. It is a small but critical step toward maintaining an equitable workplace where everyone feels valued, not to mention motivated to give their absolute best.

TWO

Mise en Place

*Why this old chef's mantra applies
to every project you undertake*

Every culinary student learns the words *mise en place*. Translated from French, they mean "putting in place" or "everything in its place."

In culinary school, it refers to the essential prep that every student needs to do: all recipe ingredients measured out, ready to be incorporated into the dish before you begin. Every cooking show you've ever seen does this—you know, those neat little glass bowls with a teaspoon of this and a tablespoon of that. Of course, there's a wide gulf between doing this in theory in an educational setting and doing it every day in a busy restaurant.

In the worst-run restaurants, you'll see that much of *mise en place* is skipped. I encounter this all the time on *Restaurant: Impossible*. The cooks will always have excuses, and of course all of them are bullshit. Because I've got news for you: The forty-five-minute delay that you encountered at that restaurant that you—of course—*never* went back to? It didn't happen because the restaurant got too busy. It happened for one of two reasons:

1. The owner tried to cut costs by keeping fewer cooks on.

2. The kitchen just wasn't ready because they didn't take their prep far enough.

It doesn't matter what you order. You shouldn't be enduring an interminable wait to get your food. "Well, it takes a long time to put a well-done steak on the plate," the cook will whine. Again, nonsense. The best restaurants will have a couple of steaks already cooked to medium at the ready that just need to be brought up to temperature.

Having everything prepped and in its place also makes work conditions safer. This is crucial in restaurants because kitchens are hot, noisy, dangerous places. There's fire. Boiling oil. Sharp blades. These are the hazards of the job, hazards we gladly accept because we're undertaking a labor of love. Every industry has its own unique hazards. If, at the end of the day, you're able to add them all up and say it's still worth it, then you're in the right place.

Of course, you still work to mitigate the risk. This is universal. In the kitchen, fewer cooks running around trying to fetch items from the pantry means a lower chance of a dangerous accident. It doesn't take much imagination to extrapolate this scenario into the wider business world. For instance, the more research you can do before crunch time, the better your big presentation is going to be. The more applicants you interview, the lower your chances of landing a dud, and the higher your chances of landing an all-star. The more time you can spend digging into the prospects of any investment, the better off you'll be.

Park Vue Soul Food Bar & Restaurant

Disorganized kitchens are a hallmark of *Restaurant: Impossible*, so I had plenty of examples to choose from for this case study. But few of those examples illustrate the point as well as the most egregious case I've come across: Park Vue Soul Food Bar & Restaurant in Buffalo, New York.

Situated in a residential neighborhood and only open Friday through Sunday, Park Vue was more of a part-time hobby for the co-owner tandem of Harrita West, a full-time banker, and her mother, Schenita Williams, a full-time teacher. But this was a hobby that lost a bundle of money and caused a ton of stress; it was $100,000 in the red—almost all of that being Schenita's retirement fund—with no hope of a turnaround. Harrita estimated that the restaurant had six months of runway left before it faced permanent shutdown.

Park Vue looked like a run-down banquet hall, a soul food restaurant without any soul. Worse, the food wasn't any good—and that was when you could get your hands on some. Wait times for simple dishes like fried ribs, fish, and mac and cheese were thirty minutes on the low end, and often pushed closer to an hour. How the hell is that even possible? Because prep didn't even begin until an order came into the kitchen. Not only did the cooks have to rummage through cupboards and fridges to get what they needed, but the kitchen was set up for failure, with Harrita and Schenita bickering over who was doing what, with no system of organizing tickets—which were frequently lost, resulting in customers getting the wrong order or nothing at all.

The disorganization extended beyond the kitchen, with Harrita haphazardly storing bills in shoeboxes. "You're a banker!" I said in shock. "If you went into the bank and asked yourself for a loan, would you give yourself one?!" Humbled, Harrita admitted, "Absolutely not."

It was painful to see because Harrita and Schenita were two of the most delightful owners I've met, with a deep desire to give back to the low-income community where they lived. Indeed, Park Vue should have been a neighborhood cornerstone, not the forgotten curiosity it had become.

I helped them develop a plan to advertise with the seven area churches, tithing back 10 percent of the proceeds they got from congregations coming in after Sunday service. With a menu revamp, renovation, and a bit of training on the benefits of prep—along with hiring some experienced kitchen help—they were well on their way to turning Park Vue into everything it could be.

"Prep is the most important thing you can do in any business," I told Harrita. "If you prep correctly, service is a breeze."

During the grand reopening, patrons didn't wait an hour for their meals. The low-end wait time was trimmed to a mere four minutes, which, for the kind of food Park Vue offered, was about right.

As I wrote earlier in this chapter, prep isn't just a necessity for restaurants but businesses of all kinds. When your customers walk through the door, they should be able to get what they came for quickly and easily. Creating a seamless customer experience is often the difference between having a one-time customer or a loyal one who will return for years to come. In short: Be ready. You don't want to have to get ready, and your customers won't wait for it, either.

HOW I GO BIG

*Why the growth of your business shouldn't
send your operation into a frenzy*

If you come into my kitchen at service time, it's always going to look the same. People moving with speed and purpose, but nobody running around looking crazed or lost or trying to do a million things at the same time. This is true if we're cooking for fifty people, five hundred, or five thousand (as we've done at a few troop benefits). Cooking for more people is obviously more work, but most of that work is absorbed in the prep phase and responsibly disbursed by my executive chefs to line cooks and sous chefs, who they've trained to deliver the same product every time.

I mention this not just because I take great pride in the harmony of the kitchen no matter how big we go, but because there's a lesson here for all businesses. Scaling up should not be a question of forgoing sleep and putting in endless hours as the deadline approaches. Once you've truly mastered your craft, you'll be able to take the goal and break it down into manageable tasks that can be delegated to team members who may not have mastery but do possess competence.

Here are some of the biggest mistakes I've seen restaurateurs make. Again, you needn't be in the restaurant industry to see the parallels to every other type of business.

- *Their menus are too big,* forcing them to keep more inventory, increasing the risk of spoilage and waste, which in turn leads to . . .

- *Panic shopping,* where members of the kitchen staff will have to go out to shop at local markets and grocery stores to get enough fresh protein and produce on hand for that day's service.

- *Lack of weekly prep,* which increases the time it takes to get a plate in front of a diner.

- *Their recipes are not written out,* which hurts consistency of the product delivered to the table; this problem increases exponentially as staff turns over and institutional knowledge is lost.

- *Recipes are not tasted regularly* after being initially delegated by the executive chef. Recipes need constant inspection, tasting, and visual examination as ingredient quality can vary and sourcing can change with the seasons. Produce, of course, can vary wildly in terms of taste, freshness, and size (don't say a recipe requires two apples or one onion when "½ cup chopped" is a much more accurate measurement), but proteins also have a wide amount of variance as no two cows, pigs, or chickens are ever exactly alike.

- *There are too many conflicting egos.* It's hard enough when you've got a tyrannical owner or executive chef. Now imagine you've got both, as well as an egotistical bartender, host, and server. It's enough to sink even a restaurant that people love.

Each mistake hurts the business in its own unique way, yet there's a common thread that runs between all of them: lack of foresight. In each situation, the owner has chosen to forgo action that could put the business ahead and instead decided to take things day-to-day, treading water and only addressing the most immediate concerns. This might work for a while, but it would only take a single, unexpectedly busy day to break the operation.

Ten times out of ten, I would always choose to be overprepared than risk just scraping by or failing a stress test. When my chefs go in to prep for a massive event—such as the aforementioned troop benefit to feed a few thousand—the prep phase begins months in advance with designing the menu, pre-planning purchase orders for all the food we'll need (which requires a lot of math, hence all my chefs are pretty good at handling a spreadsheet), and securing enough kitchen volunteers to get all the prep work done.

By the time the day arrives, the prep has paid off and has all been worth it. An army of volunteers works with precision and harmony, and it's truly breathtaking to see all the plates go out and watch such a large number of people all receive hot, gourmet food in a matter of minutes. That's where the right prep can get you. Thousands fed in seamless fashion. Harmony out of chaos.

Now, let's focus on the last item on the list—conflicting egos.

My name is on the ticket and the menu, my face is on the billboard, and the recipes are mine, hence it's a "Robert Irvine" event. But let's not be ridiculous. I've illustrated that you can't do this kind of work by yourself and shown how many helping hands and skilled lieutenants you need to pull it off. So when I step into the kitchen on the day, I don't say to my executive chefs, "OK, I'm here, so you can step aside now." I say, "How can I help?" And I mean it—if there's something that needs prepping or taste-testing to help keep us on schedule, I'm at their disposal.

So many leaders would think that a move like that would be a sign of weakness. Bullshit. Checking your ego and not being threatened by your subordinates is not only a sign of strength; it's a vote of confidence in the people you hired that empowers them and invests them in the outcome. When they succeed because you put them in a position to succeed and then got out of their way, they become more self-assured, ambitious, and—best of all—more capable of handling bigger and bigger projects. I cannot impress upon you enough how important it is that as you scale your operations, you're giving your lieutenants room to learn and grow. They will be your most valuable assets going forward. Be certain to treat them as such.

Training staff for restaurants is more than a matter of making sure that each cook possesses the necessary skills for a specific job. You also need to make sure they can pay attention—specifically to the unique nature of every new batch of ingredients that's delivered. Take steak, for example. We know that no two steaks are ever exactly alike. You might be purchasing the best of the best—Kobe beef or USDA prime—but each one of those pieces of meat will have its own unique marbling, texture, and, ultimately, flavor. The same goes for a head of lettuce, a basket of mushrooms, or a bushel of corn. These differences can sometimes be subtle, and they can sometimes be significant. What the well-trained cook recognizes is that all these differences are *meaningful* and that all of them can be worked with. The effect of an inferior product can be mitigated. The effect of a superior product can be enhanced. What matters in the end is the overall dish.

Customers will never see what the cook had to do to bring them the final plate—be it staying out of the way of the perfect cut of meat or working their ass off to make a subpar cut more palatable. All they see is the finished product. This has a direct analog in every other type of business, and I'm certain that learning to be flexible in the face of so many variables in the kitchen is what made me a better businessman. The ability to see obstacles not as a random occurrence of misfortune but as an opportunity to learn, grow, and improve is essential if you're to have any hope of succeeding in the long term.

Getting to a point with your people where you trust them implicitly is a process, of course, but it all begins with the right training. Here's how I do it.

Training Your Staff

Why the "kitchen sink" approach never works—and what you need to do instead

Simply put, start by training specialties. Don't teach everything at once if it's not necessary. You might eventually need the chef working the pizza station to have the flexibility to go work the grill or go to the back to make a pastry, but if they're starting at the pizza station, just teach that. When learning new skills, it helps to be able to focus on mastering a small handful of instructions. You might think you're being more efficient and saving time by training the whole staff in a full-day seminar type of setting, but in my experience, retention of information wanes after just a couple short hours of instruction, and most of your staff will wind up needing to be taught again. Or worse, they'll act like they've mastered it out of fear of negative feedback, and they'll carry on doing things the wrong way.

Test (or sample) everything they do—and require that they do the same. This isn't just essential for ensuring you're putting the best possible product on the plate; it eliminates waste and allows your staff to fully appreciate what it is they're doing. If your employees love what they're making, your customers will, too. You can walk right up and ask for a taste or, preferably, you can just sit for a service and see what happens. In non-restaurant settings, the approach is the same: stand back and let your employees do their thing without being watched, then inspect at the end.

SCALING UP

Basic recipes are not infinitely scalable—
going bigger requires a new formula

There's an old buttermilk pancake recipe I learned when I was a kid that was, and remains, one of the best things I've ever cooked. It was wildly simple: a cup of flour, a pinch of salt and baking soda, an egg, a couple of tablespoons of melted butter, and a little more than a cup of buttermilk. Whip it up, ladle it onto a hot griddle, and a couple of minutes later you're eating some of the best pancakes you've ever had in your life.

The first time or two, I did this while referring to the recipe at every step. By the third time, I could do it from memory; as it is with so many recipes, it's been like riding a bike ever since. There's no chance I could ever forget how to make those pancakes even if I tried. If I'm cooking for a few more people than normal, no problem: I just double the recipe. A small crowd? Triple it. But by the time you need to quadruple or quintuple a recipe . . . well, the math doesn't hold up anymore.

All of a sudden, the batter is unwieldy. The typical household mixing bowl proves to be too small, the amount of flour requires more mixing to incorporate, and by the time I've combined it with the wet ingredients, the batter just doesn't look the same. So what the hell happened? The problem is scale. Most recipes are not infinitely scalable. Things happen at the molecular level that throw a wrench into your plans. In this case, the wheat gluten becomes too stressed from the extra mixing and the batter becomes rubbery like gum instead of thick and fluffy. The solution might be to add a bit more buttermilk. Of course, if you do that, you have to add a bit more salt and baking soda to maintain balance. Oh, wait . . . if you do that, you might need a little more butter. And do you still have enough egg? Oh no! We're not "sticking to the recipe"!

In this situation, you have a few options:

1. Plow ahead and try to stick with the same exact recipe, risking the fact that you might wind up with something that's *similar* to your original intent but not quite the same product. Not bad, per se, but not up to your standards.

2. Batch it out. You know the recipe works fine when doubled, so you just do that two or three times. It's a lot more work and takes a hell of a lot longer, but at least you know you're going to nail the finished product.

3. You recognize that Option 1 is out of the question and Option 2 takes too damn long, so you remember that you've got something called experience, and thanks to this experience you know what the thing is supposed to look and taste like. So after a glance at the batter and a quick taste test, you know whether or not you need to make adjustments and what they should be. You know what perfect is, so you tinker here and there until you nail it. You avoid putting out a substandard dish and you're able to do so without adding a lot of time to the process.

I don't know about you, but I want Option 3. I want to figure out a new and better way. I'll write down what I do so I needn't go through the tinkering and exploration again, and by the end I'll have a new recipe for buttermilk pancakes (large scale). In any situation where you have a wealth of experience to draw from, Option 3 ought to be what you go for.

And yet...

So many chefs—unwilling to take risks or trust their instincts—will go for Option 1 or 2, considering them to be safer but ultimately hurting themselves and their customers in the process.

There's a lesson here for every type of growing business. You can't expand if you insist on doing everything exactly the same way as you grow. (This would be like choosing Option 1 in the recipe example.) And you'll never reach your expansion goals if your quality control measures demand that you make each product one at a time. (This would be like choosing Option 2.)

Your only chance, then, at a healthy and successful expansion lies in relying on your experience, and the instincts and taste you've developed to get to this point. You know what the finished product should be. *So keep an eye on it.* Taste test. Add another pinch of this and that. Constantly inspect and reevaluate the situation. Ask plenty of questions of your lieutenants and new hires. And listen to your inner monologue. What is your gut telling you? I'm willing to wager that you're already in possession of the right answers. To get to those answers, you'll need to clear your head, focus on what's in front of you, and be honest about what you see. The business owner with an intimate knowledge of the tiny details—and a firm grasp of the bigger picture—is a business owner who can meet any challenge.

A Pizza Melody

Going big or scaling up can take many different forms. It can mean expansion into multiple locations, expanding the footprint of your current location, increasing the number or volume of product offerings, delivering to new territories, and swelling the ranks of your workforce. In the case of George Felter, owner of A Pizza Melody in Las Vegas, his ambitions had outpaced his ability. After initially buying a small pizzeria that could seat fifteen people with his husband, Terry Schlitter, he expanded the restaurant's footprint, more than doubling in size. This required more employees and inexplicably, in George's mind, an enormous menu to match, about a hundred items by my count. This made food costs—and waste—skyrocket. How bad did it get? By the time I visited for our Season 17 episode of *Restaurant: Impossible*, George's foray into the pizza business had lost over $900,000. Terry's job at the airport was the only thing keeping the restaurant afloat.

Why did it get this bad? Well, there were a lot of issues George needed to address. First and foremost, he was visibly angry most of the time, and would verbally explode on his manager Ericka and head chef Jerome at the drop of a dime. The root of the anger: He had grown up as a gay man in a born-again Christian household that would never have accepted him if he came out. Hiding his true self for years, he married a woman and had three sons. The weight of living a lie throughout twenty-six years of marriage finally crushed him. Though he found love and support with Terry, the bitterness of essentially losing his sons in the divorce sent him into a spiral.

On the business side of things, that anger clouded his judgment and made him immune to criticism and new ideas; this caused unnecessary setbacks because his chef and manager were highly creative, talented, and capable people, but couldn't bring any of those positive forces to bear on their work. For instance, when I sat for a service, I really disliked the food I was served, but when I went back into the kitchen and asked Jerome to make me something, anything, that came from his heart, he made me a wonderful dish of Chicken Milanese with a summer salad and English pea puree. George's micromanaging—and subsequent outbursts when things didn't go his way—made it impossible for his employees to take creative risks that could lead to a positive breakthrough like that. Almost every episode of *Restaurant: Impossible* contains a cautionary tale about micromanaging, but George's management style was detrimental for another reason: Jerome was responsible for putting out the hundred menu items George had chosen, diminishing the restaurant's core competency, the thing they ought to have been known for in the area, which, naturally, was pizza.

I took a marker and wrote down on dinner plates the names of all the menu items that were lousy sellers. "If it hasn't sold in thirty days, it doesn't belong on your menu," I told George. I then asked George to smash all those plates outside. It was a memorable lesson and a cathartic release—an outlet for George's considerable anger and pain. This one small step helped start the process of purging that poisonous fury from his life, and from there, healing could begin.

"Your life set you up for where you are, but it doesn't have to keep going in that direction," I told him, and as that truth landed on him, he exploded in tears.

As for the much larger space he had taken on in the hope of drawing bigger crowds, we found a way to make it much more inviting, lengthening the bar and turning their karaoke stage (hence the name A Pizza Melody) into a place where people would actually want to spend a lot of time. After we left, sales went up 50 percent and the restaurant could pay its own bills without Terry's help. With Ericka in charge of the front of house and Jerome firmly in control of the kitchen, George and Terry are now frequently seen enjoying the karaoke bar.

The work to make A Pizza Melody a lasting success will be ongoing, of course, but without stripping down the menu to its essentials—and removing the roadblocks that had bloated it in the first place—that work couldn't have even begun.

As you look at your own product offerings, always keep core competency in the forefront of your mind. Ask yourself: What is my business best at? What do we want to be known for? As you look to add products, services, employees, physical space, or an additional location, ask whether that expansion serves your mission. If it doesn't, or if you feel like you might be reaching, you're probably better off focusing on the fundamentals.

Opening a Restaurant

Everything you need to develop—from culinary skills
to business planning to inspecting your real estate

If you want to open a restaurant, there's lot of prep you need to do—inside and outside the kitchen. First, I know it sounds insane that I need to point this out at all—but you need to be sure you can really cook. Just because your friends and family tell you that you're great doesn't mean anything. So you've got some good recipes and you can cook for five to ten people. Well, a lot of folks can do that, and most of them shouldn't be opening a restaurant. It would be akin to singing your infant to sleep and thinking you should win *American Idol*. You need to remember that doing this thing every day for a lot of people is a very different proposition than doing it in the comfort of your home. Cook for test groups who don't have a vested interest in telling you that you're good because they don't want to hurt your feelings. Better yet, take a job in a real restaurant.

Once you've established you've actually got some skills, your work is just beginning. Where is this restaurant going? Into a preexisting building? Are you ready to inspect every corner of the facility from the roof to the foundation and make sure you won't have tens or hundreds of thousands of dollars' worth of repairs on your hands six months after you buy it?

Are you ready to do the demographic research for the area where you want to put this thing? You love your hometown and you always thought it should have a high-end steakhouse experience. OK, but what's the median income in your hometown? Never mind interest—will the residents even be able to afford it? Will you be able to recruit the kind of talent required to keep such a place open and operating at a high standard?

Now, let's say you've answered all these questions and are satisfied with the answers. You're moving into a great building in an awesome area that is dying for the kind of place you want to open. Congrats! But I've got new questions for you: What are you going to do with that dish that isn't selling? Are you willing to omit it from the menu? Or change it? Even if you consider it your signature dish? The thing that you're best at? The thing you think you should be known for?

"But this is an old family recipe!"

Trust me, I can tell. It tastes . . . antiquated. I'm not being mean. I'm being real. Just because it brings you comfort to have that dish when your family gets together for the holidays doesn't mean anything. The public's palate is an ever-changing thing. As our world shrinks and we're constantly exposed to new things, everyone's tastes evolve and become more sophisticated. What worked in the past is not guaranteed to work today.

Consumer choice is another thing that has changed rapidly alongside palates. How many restaurants did your hometown have when you were growing up? A half dozen? Maybe less? Maybe your concept would have kicked ass in that environment. But with ten times that amount competing for customers, will it still stand out?

As you face these questions, you might think that I'm being too hard. Most of the restaurateurs I visit on *Restaurant: Impossible* think the same thing. All these folks wind up thanking me and wishing they had asked these questions before they poured their life savings into a failing business. Ask these questions of yourself and be honest with the answers. You'll thank me, too.

SHORTCUTS CAN BE FATAL

*Sometimes, no product is better
than a substandard one*

". . . and that's how you make your brine. Just drop the chicken in there, and twenty-four hours from now, it's ready."

"Got it."

"Great. Now here's what you do after it's done brining . . ."

This is a very brief excerpt from a typical training session in a kitchen. Executive chef shows the kitchen staff how something needs to be done. They learn it, demonstrate an ability to do it, produce a finished product up to the same standard as the executive chef, and . . . we're done here, right?

Not by a long shot. Unfortunately, many chefs would think that once a cook demonstrates aptitude, the work is finished. But ability doesn't equal consistency, let alone mastery.

So what happens next? Well, in most cases, once the executive chef has taught something to the staff, they write it off and don't think about it again. Meanwhile, the kitchen staff encounters a day when they're harried—maybe a combination of a busy night and being short-staffed. Happens often enough. So, they start to cut corners. That twenty-four-hour brine gets cut down to eighteen hours, or twelve. The finished product tastes good—close enough, anyway—but the murmurs among the customers begin:

"Chicken sandwich is . . . *pretty good*, right? . . . I thought it was better last time. It's a little chewy today . . ."

And in that moment, a five-star word-of-mouth review—from someone who was so passionate about your restaurant that they were evangelizing on your behalf and bringing in new customers—becomes a three-and-a-half-star review. Thanks to that shortcut, "It's amazing! You have to go!" has now become "It's OK. They were better when they first opened . . ."

This is a microcosm of the typical slow death that so many restaurants experience. Customers have such an incredible wealth of choice in this industry that you can't afford to give them a pretty good or average experience. Which means you can't afford to take shortcuts with your processes. If the recipe says the meat needs to be brined for twenty-four hours, then brine the damn thing for twenty-four hours. If time constraints or other unforeseen circumstances prevent this from happening, take it off the menu for a night! While maybe not ideal, it's better than serving up something that will diminish your reputation. You can't afford that, because reputation is all you really have. In the long run, this tactic might even help. When the server says, "I'm so sorry, but we're out of that tonight," you wind up with a temporarily disappointed customer, but on another level you've conveyed a sense of exclusivity around your product.

Moreover, you've further differentiated yourself from your competition because, hey, your thing is so good you can't even get it every day! We live in a world where people can get unlimited amounts of anything they want at any moment, from movies and music to food and drink. In such an environment, offering people something that is not just superior in quality but of limited availability is a strong power play.

LEADING THROUGH CRISIS

How Hard Times Can Create Stronger Businesses

As soon as I had the concept for this book set and began to sit down to write it, the coronavirus pandemic upended our lives. A few months into the pandemic, Comcast Business—a longtime partner of mine—asked if I would deliver the keynote address at their Future of Business Virtual Conference. I tried to focus not just on how to survive the pandemic but on how to use the lessons of the pandemic to prepare for future disruptions to the way we live and do business. Because I think its message holds up for the post-pandemic world, I'm happy to share the text of my speech here.

WHATEVER BUSINESS YOU'RE IN, COVID caused you to face new, unique challenges that you never imagined before.

As a business owner, preparing for the worst needs to be a top priority—even in the best of times. Because you all know that rapid change due to advancing technology, disruption from upstart competitors, and constantly shifting customer expectations—these are permanent terms of doing business.

You've all met people who shrink in the face of a challenge, and those who are excited to meet it. Those who wish it away, and those who become more focused when the stakes are raised and more obstacles pile up.

Moments of crisis reveal who a person really is.

And in business, moments of crisis reveal how healthy a company really is, what kind of leadership it has, and how seriously it takes potential threats that have yet to enter the public consciousness.

If you look at every business that pushed through the early stages of the coronavirus pandemic, that gives you a good idea of how prepared or responsive they'll be to a security breach, a financial crisis, and general disruption in the marketplace.

I had to close my restaurants to the public just like everyone else, but I didn't let what we couldn't do get in the way of what we could do.

Which brings me to a quote I'd like to share with you: "Always render more and better service of you, no matter what the task may be."

Og Mandino, the founder of *Success Magazine*, said that. It was a principle he lived by—the notion that if you simply focus on providing value to people's lives, the rewards—monetary or otherwise—will eventually find you, even if it's not in direct relation to that service.

When the pandemic hit, the Irvine family of brands immediately began focusing on exactly that question: How can we add value to people's lives?

The chefs who work for me began whipping up dozens of recipes to share with people who were newly homebound and scraping through their cupboards to cook a decent meal for their families at a time when not only was everyone confused about how safe it was to go out to get groceries, but they also encountered empty shelves when they did venture out.

The Robert Irvine Foundation issued grants to provide mental health and wellness services to first responders while my protein bar company, FitCrunch, donated over twenty-four thousand protein bars to hospitals, military bases, and first responders.

My distillery, Boardroom Spirits in Lansdale, Pennsylvania, immediately began manufacturing and giving away bottles of hand sanitizer—one thousand gallons in total. At the same time—and for the first time ever—we began home delivery of our products. There was no purchase necessary to get the hand sanitizer, but the gesture of goodwill—along with the convenience we offered to our customers—resulted in this: in the month of April 2020, we sold as much vodka, gin, whiskey, rum, and tequila as we did in all of 2019.

For everyone on my team, this time has been a powerful learning experience. Much of this action didn't yield directly related financial results, but we provided value to people's lives, and I'm a firm believer that if we do one good deed for someone today, our world will be better tomorrow. On some level, people recognized what we were doing, and as a result we are collectively in a stronger position today than we were before the onset of COVID-19.

You might say, "Well, that's fine for you—you're fortunate that your products are diversified." Nonsense. The Irvine family of businesses is not totally unique. Every business that has been able to thrive during this time has a similar story to tell. Whether it was quickly implementing curbside pickup and delivery, employing new safety measures to ensure that customers felt totally comfortable, or utilizing tech to connect with the public virtually, successful businesses all shared common best practices that have nothing to do with their product offerings or the specificity of the coronavirus pandemic. Follow these keys, and your business will be prepared to face the next crisis, whatever it may be.

Best Practice #1: Don't Panic

Panic is a natural reaction to danger. It's your body preparing you for fight or flight. But no one can afford to stay in the panicked state. You need to take that panic and use it to your advantage. Allow it to sharpen your focus and spur meaningful action.

Best Practice #2:
Stay Engaged with Your Customers

Social media is—to make an understatement—many things. Too often it seems like we're talking about it because it's filled with negativity and misinformation and it can wreak havoc on our civil discourse. But for businesses with good message discipline, it's still the most powerful tool we have to stay connected to our customers. Yes, you still need a good website, but that's for customers who already made the decision to go and find you. By maintaining social channels across all the major platforms, you're making it easier to stay on your customers' minds by finding them where they are—where they're increasingly choosing to spend more and more of their time.

The most successful companies engage on social media not just by alerting the public to an upcoming sale or announcing a new item, but by sharing quality free content, spreading a generally positive message, and encouraging the audience to speak up and join the conversation.

Since I began to use social media some years ago, spreading a positive message was natural for me because it was an extension of what people were seeing from me on TV. I've refined it over the years, and it's never been more handy than in the past six months as everyone turned in unison to their screens. It allowed all my companies to share a motivational message and let people know how we were helping those in need. We experienced higher engagement, brand awareness, and channel growth during this time than at any point in our history.

Best Practice #3:
Engage with Your Employees

I'm typically on the road for about three hundred days a year. My team reflects that. I collect people—the best and brightest from my travels. That means I have employees in San Antonio, Philadelphia, New York, Tampa, and many places in between.

During a crisis, my first order of business is to make the rounds with all of them. Check in and make sure that they and their families are safe and to see how they are doing. This sounds so simple, but you'd be shocked by how many business leaders don't do it. They assume everything is OK unless they hear otherwise from their employees. You can never assume.

You need to do this often, not just when a crisis arises—and not just because it's the right thing to do. It's the right thing for your business. When your employees are facing serious issues, it will quickly affect performance. Hence, their issues become your issues.

Best Practice #4: Secure Your Data

When it comes to cybersecurity software and backup protocols, there are two ways of approaching it: stay on the bleeding edge of the absolute best. Or: have nothing at all. Outdated software and websites that are highly vulnerable to attacks—or, worse, use a public portal for employee sign-ins—aren't just liabilities. They are targets on your back.

Downloading and installing every software update for everything you're running can seem time-consuming and tedious, but it's important, and can serve to patch most vulnerabilities in your system.

Best Practice #5: Be Prepared

This final point is rather broad and intentionally so.

What I mean by "be prepared" is that you need to use your imagination to think of worst-case scenarios and how they could affect your business. "Be prepared" encompasses everything from making sure you're well-stocked in case there's a disruption in the supply chain to considering how you're going to move product if the government suddenly says that people may not enter your store.

Case in point: A few weeks ago, the Robert Irvine Foundation issued a grant to a small, veteran-owned ice cream parlor in Williamsport, Pennsylvania, to help them stay afloat. Like every other business in the area, they were forced to close their doors at the onset of the pandemic. Unlike other eateries that could continue to serve through drive-through or walk-up windows, they didn't have anything like that. And when they applied to build one, they were rejected because local authorities were trying to limit variables; unless the drive-through or walk-up window was preexisting, you were not allowed to use it during this time.

This story is also a great case study in the importance of being fully up-to-date on government regulations everywhere you do business. Can you afford to pay the costs of renovations only to discover halfway through that you've suddenly run afoul of the law?

Now, with the help of the Robert Irvine Foundation and government assistance, it looks like this ice cream parlor is going to make it. But use it as a lesson and think hard right now. What is your version of the walk-up window? If people couldn't enter your place of business, how would you serve them? If another airborne pandemic comes to our shores, do you have a stockpile of personal protective equipment so your employees can continue working safely? Can you deliver products directly to customers? Can customers buy your products and services through the most popular apps and social media channels?

I'm not trying to worry you into a frenzy. Of course, there's that old saying that worry is using your imagination to create something you don't want. I'd rather you always imagine the best outcome. But it is incumbent upon every business leader to be aware of potential problem areas and address them in their theoretical state before they manifest into real problems that threaten the future of your business.

In closing, I want you to remember that no one can predict the future. If anyone could tell you exactly what's coming, they wouldn't be a business consultant—they'd be a fortune-teller.

Thankfully, you don't need to know the future to survive—and thrive—in an unforeseen crisis. You need to prepare for the worst, hope for the best, and lead your employees and customers by example with a persistent attitude of positive expectation.

And above all, remember to stay close to the action! You can't insulate yourself from what's happening on the ground. If you can't be in your actual place of business, communicate frequently with the folks who are running your day-to-day operations. Listen closely to what they have to say—but measure everything you can with hard data. Great employees that you trust are key. But even they might try to paint a rosier picture for you than what the reality is.

Data, on the other hand, won't try to spare your feelings. Sales figures and customer feedback are hard facts. The business leaders who remember this and stay ready to pivot to new ground are the ones who can succeed in any situation.

Success in business isn't easy. Hard work and determination are key, but they don't guarantee victory.

However, if you can combine these elements with the best practices I've mentioned, a trusted workforce, good data, and a willingness to adapt to uncontrollable circumstances, you have all the ingredients you need to achieve any goal.

Thank you for listening. In parting, I ask that you please remember the words that I try to live by every day: nothing is impossible.

THREE

It's Not Their Job to Get It

It's your job to sell it

I was leaving a meeting with CBS a few years ago. I had just pitched a new show in which I would help struggling small business owners turn their fortunes around. Similar in concept to *Restaurant: Impossible* but minus the culinary aspect, I had hoped it would mark an interesting but natural brand extension—something I was sure audiences were ready to watch.

The executives seemed intrigued, and I felt good about where I had left things. Then a day went by. Then a few. Then a week. Then a couple of weeks.

My agent pinged me and told me he'd follow up with the network. *Sure*, I told him. *Do that*. It's his job, after all, to do such things. But he didn't need to call anyone to figure out what I had already figured out. They were a no. I've had enough experience in this business to know that if they're not beating down your door with an offer, then the interest just isn't there, regardless of what they told you in the meeting. Typically, the lack of an answer is your answer.

This is part of "taking an L," as I wrote about in the introduction. By the time anyone has forged a successful television or film career, they have been tempered in the molten-hot fires of rejection. I learned that the most important thing about rejection is how you frame it, because that's going to directly impact how quickly you can get back up and try again or apply your talents to something new.

In the case of the CBS pitch, after a few months of not hearing from the network, I ran into an old friend. We caught up about this and that, and he asked me if I had recently pitched anything new. I told him about the concept but that the network had passed.

"Jeez, that's a great idea!" my friend said. "They didn't see it, huh? What stiffs."

I know he was trying to be supportive and wanted to show that he was in my corner. But in my mind, he had it backward. When you're trying to sell something—whether it's a new show to a network or a sandwich to a guy on his lunch break—it's not the prospective customer's job to understand. It's your job to *make* them understand. Nor is it their job to devote their full attention to you and absorb everything you're saying; it's your job to demand their attention with a sales pitch that's so compelling it can't be ignored.

Then, if you don't make the sale, it's not because they're too dense to understand how great they could have had it if only they'd bought from you; it's because you failed to break through. Whether you didn't appeal to their immediate needs with your particular product offering or you failed to connect with them on an emotional level, the responsibility lies solely with you.

Bullshit, you say. *Let's be real: Some customers/vendors/buyers just aren't that bright. If they don't get it, that's not my fault.*

Fair enough, but I'm not defaulting to the old adage about the customer always being right so that I can sell you some pablum about trying harder. *Rise and grind*, as the kids say. I'm saying that once you take full responsibility for whatever happens, positive or negative, you are now in possession of all the power in whatever room you go into.

Let's go back to TV pitching again, since it's one of the most notoriously competitive and unforgiving scenarios where anyone could be asked to sell. And now let's go with two of my pitches that did work out—*Dinner: Impossible* and *Restaurant: Impossible*. In both of those scenarios, I was convinced of a singular vision of what the shows should be. I knew the structure and what the emotional journey of each episode would feel like, and it allowed me to tell that story in a clear and concise manner. I didn't walk into the room worrying about what each person would think and *oh no, what if I lose them somewhere in the middle of my presentation or what if they're tired of these challenge/makeover shows or* . . . I put it all out of my head. I took the power away from them and vested all of it in myself.

The moment you do that, there's a dramatic shift in the dynamic. Because someone who's pitching anything and worried about losing the sale immediately comes off as desperate, and there's nothing any buyer—of TV shows or sandwiches—likes less than a salesperson who seems like they might starve if you don't hand over your money.

Keeping that power fully vested in yourself even when your pitch fails—as mine did with CBS—allows you to keep going without missing a beat. Think about it: Why would I keep trying if I'm fully dependent on other people? If I thought that way, then I'm no longer selling something. I'm just hunting for the person who will get it immediately. Well, I don't know who that person is or where they work, and if I'm dependent on a totally perfect scenario like that, I may as well just buy lotto tickets. I have no interest in a life where other people are in charge of my destiny with final say over what I can and can't do. I could keep pitching with that in mind, but I'd be like a blind mole, crawling around trying to sniff out a meal. If instead I say, "OK, that didn't work. How can I make my next pitch even better?" then I'm operating from a position of real power, and it is very difficult indeed to keep down a person who possesses such an attitude.

All of us in the business world, whether we realize it or not, signed up for a sales job. You are always selling.

It's an important fact to remember, so write it down on the whiteboard in your office. Or on a sticky note and put it next to your bed. Or on a slip of paper and tuck it into your wallet. Or tattoo the damn thing to the inside of your eyelids, because guess what? You are always selling.

But Robert, what about when I'm just having a friendly conversation with a customer?

Didn't you hear me? I said you're *always* selling. The feeling your customer leaves with after that conversation will inform their decision to come back or go somewhere else. Hence, like it or not, you were selling.

But what about when I'm—

Enough! I said you're always selling and I meant it.

Everything you do contributes—positively or negatively—to your ability to do business. Every. Single. Behavior. The cleanliness—or lack thereof—of your establishment communicates to your customers whether you care or not. Hence, keeping it tidy is an act of salesmanship. Your customers' ability to easily find information about you online—be it menus, prices, parking, hours of operation, FAQs, where you source product from—is an act of salesmanship. If your to-go bags and business cards are high-quality materials and look clean and professional, that's an act of salesmanship.

You are always selling. Your products. Your ideas. Your whole self. How you comport yourself in all your daily interactions with employees, clients, and peers is an act of salesmanship, because the way you act is an advertisement to keep working with you or run the other way, to dive in and invest more time and money in what you're doing, or to cut losses and bounce.

Don't think of the "always selling" mantra as a burden, but as one more way to keep the center of power within yourself. It's never out there. It's always in here.

SALESMANSHIP

It's not the smarmy magic act we've grown wary of

I've done a good job of honing my skills as a salesman over the years. And I don't just mean delivering a polished pitch on QVC, which I do from time to time. I mean selling in a room. Sitting down with CEOs and buyers for companies like Wal-Mart and Amazon and spinning a grand yarn about why they need to have my products on their shelves, or pitching a TV show as I wrote about in the previous section.

But with age and experience has come the realization that there is no better salesman than data. When you're able to walk into a room and say, "Buy this protein bar because we have a 4.7/5 rating on Amazon with over three thousand reviews," that's always going to be more powerful than any song and dance I could do about how the bars are baked or personally developed in my kitchen, or utilize only the highest-quality ingredients, and blah, blah, blah.

The decision makers at big companies didn't get to where they are by going with their gut. They don't write fat checks because gosh darn it that salesperson guessed their age to be fifteen years younger than it really was. (Why does that happen all the time? Oh, I dunno . . . maybe because most salespeople are full of shit!) Yes, being good at sales is important and can get you over the finish line, but it's only the last 10 percent of what you need. The best executives want to make an informed decision, and to do that they need data.

If you're just starting out, you might throw up your hands at this point. What kind of data and sales figures can you point to if you haven't launched the damn thing yet? Isn't this just another version of the old catch-22: can't get a job without experience, and can't get experience without a job? Not quite. Data can come in many forms. While you might not be able to just drop a trump card about massive sales figures or thousands of online reviews, you can quantify your product in other ways. If it's unique, don't just say so. Prove it.

Let's say you've got an artisanal chocolate mousse. It's been selling great in your tiny storefront and at the local farmers' markets. Now you're trying to convince a regional grocer to carry it in-store. Great. Now you need to quantify everything about the customer response.

- How quickly does a fresh batch sell out?

- How many eggs, pounds of sugar, and gallons of heavy cream do you go through every week? (This might seem like a background detail to you, but it offers

other people perspective about how much business
you do.)

• How many repeat customers do you have?

• What are customers saying about the product in
person?

Write it all down! Everything you see, hear, and do in your
day-to-day operations can be transformed into data that makes
a buyer—or potential investor—feel a lot better about opening
their checkbook. You just need to put yourself in that person's
shoes and reimagine everything you experience as a set of numbers that can be exploited to make the sale. For someone who is
exclusively focused on product quality, this can be hard to do,
but it's far from impossible. It just requires a mindset shift.

On my team, I'm fortunate enough to have a few people who
do this extraordinarily well. They're committed to product
quality and understand how to develop an emotional connection between consumers and products, but they also know how
to break everything down into data.

Let's say we're talking about one of the frozen dishes offered
by Robert Irvine Foods, Creole Barbecue Glazed Atlantic
Salmon. If I'm talking to someone who's interested in that product, I can turn to my VP of finance, Josh Lingenfelter, who
knows the weight of each palette of frozen fish off the top of his
head. He also knows how many pennies per palette we could
save if we used a slightly thinner cardboard box and can quickly
extrapolate that figure over the course of a year or a decade at
varying sell rates to let us know what we're looking at. If I want
a different variable—let's say we want to now ship the fish with

green beans instead of mixed vegetables—it wouldn't take him long to tell me what that looks like.

This is a serious talent—you could call it high-performance accounting—and most number crunchers can't quite do it the way he can. So while you might not be able to fall back on a Josh of your own, you can learn to think like him. You can start by adopting this mantra: everything you do matters. It's true in life, in relationships, in fitness, and in business. Know that every decision you make about how to spend your time, what hours your business will keep, how much inventory to have on hand—every single one of those decisions is subject to a cost-benefit analysis. If you're honest and thorough in that analysis, that's a terrific start. It might not be as good as having classic business training or an MBA like Josh has, but it's an important part of the puzzle. In the beginning, it may all seem like a jumble of disconnected details. After a while in the trenches, though, you begin to see the world like Neo in *The Matrix*—everything around you is just data. And in your case, all that data has a dollar value.

To bring it back to salesmanship: while it may be a smaller piece of the puzzle than many people think, it still has tremendous value. And in certain instances—like when you're caught off-guard and don't have data to reinforce your point—it can steer you out of trouble and keep a deal from falling through. If you don't like the idea of being a salesperson or are just uncomfortable with the concept, reframe it and call it what it really is: storytelling.

If you're truly passionate about what it is you're selling and can tell a story about why you love your product and your company, you don't need to avail yourself of any slick tricks you might associate with selling. Real passion—coupled with the courage and honesty to put that out in the open—is rare, and people will respond to it. Even if your story doesn't land with your audience on an emotional level, your authenticity won't go unnoticed or unappreciated. Just lay it all out there and let the chips fall where they may. More often than not, I think, you're going to be happy with the result.

On the topic of honesty, the old maxim about it being the best policy holds true in a general sense, but it becomes even more important when your pitch bottoms out. Picture this: you've told your story, presented your data (such as it is), and overcome the customer's objections. Now it's finally time to make the sale . . . except they've got one last question. And this question? Ho boy, it really undercuts your whole pitch.

In fact, the concern that has been raised in this final question leaves you convinced on the spot that not only is this product not for them but it's probably the last thing they should be buying.

How on earth was this not their first *question?* you ask yourself.

Now you're in quite a pickle, yeah?

No. You're fine. The moment the customer raises a concern that you realize might actually hurt their bottom line, there's perfect clarity in that moment. You drop all pretense of being a salesperson and you become bluntly honest with them. You underscore the risks of buying this particular product and spell out how badly it might go for them if they plowed ahead with the purchase.

It might hurt in the moment, but it accomplishes a few things in your favor. First, it's the right thing to do and allows anyone with an active conscience to sleep at night. The moral righteousness of this move isn't particularly helpful to your business at the moment, but in a theme that recurs in other sections of this book, if you can't do it for the right reasons, by all means do it for cold, calculating reasons. So, why is brutal honesty the right business move? Simple: It builds trust. Your honesty at this stage will likely result in the loss of the sale. But the next time you have something new to sell and come back around to that same customer, your honesty will be the thing in the forefront of their minds. They'll be grateful for that fact, more eager to hear your pitch, and be all the more inclined to buy from you when you're done. Remember: You can shear a sheep a million times, but only skin it once. And the more dishonesty you become comfortable with in the name of making money, the more likely you are to get tripped up on your own bullshit. The "tangled web we weave" can get incredibly confusing to the teller; before you know it you're trying to remember what you said to who and when you said it (*Oh jeez, I'd better not say this to that person, because she's going to talk with so-and-so next week, and on and on*). The easiest thing to remember is the truth. It's simple, practical, handy, and the best choice for building fruitful, long-term relationships.

Last, you need to be able to recognize when you, as the salesperson, need to say no. A screenwriter friend of mine has been asked to work on a lot of different, exciting projects over the course of his career. Established intellectual properties that will get made no matter what—which is a big deal to a screenwriter, a strange profession where you can have a career and make a decent living without any of your projects ever actually getting made. Think of screenwriting as the R&D process in Hollywood. Getting a story on paper is the first and cheapest step in the movie development process, so they get lots of different things on paper and then see if they can use that story to attract talent: actors, directors, and so on. And they often strike out. So when a screenwriter gets a chance to write a movie that is guaranteed to get made, it's a very big deal.

Yet this guy has said no to these offers more often than he has said yes. I was initially baffled, but the way he explained it made perfect sense: these producers are reaching out to him because he has a reputation as a great writer, but in his mind he's never been a good enough writer to deliver an amazing job if his whole heart wasn't into the project. It might seem tempting to go through the motions, try to muster some part of himself that's interested in the story or characters, but it would ultimately be a finished product below his standards because he only has access to his full arsenal of creative faculties when he's absolutely on fire to tell a story. He's not an expert on all stories, he tells me. He's only an expert on *his* stories.

Again we touch on this recurring theme: choosiness isn't just an appropriate ethical stand—it's good for business! Because let's say he takes that big paycheck to write *Transformers 9*. His bank account got bigger, but what happens to his long-term reputation when the movie gets critically panned and word starts to spread that he's lost a step and is only taking easy money now? That formulaic genre romps (don't get me wrong, I happen to enjoy plenty of these, but they're not exactly known for the writing, are they?) are all he can handle now and he's lost the stomach to tell more serious stories? On top of that, what happens to his morale as he sits down at the keyboard every day for months, trying to force himself to do work he fundamentally doesn't care about?

I'm not naïve. I understand that in the beginning of your entrepreneurial career you might have to say yes to more projects than you'd care to. To get the bills paid, you may find yourself developing products or delivering for customers you wish you never had to associate with. But as soon as you have the freedom to be a bit choosy, you should jump on the opportunity.

Just as in the earlier example of the restaurant that takes an item off the menu for a night when it doesn't have the right ingredient quality or necessary prep time, you can create an air of exclusivity around yourself and your services by saying no at the right times. Saying yes to everything makes you common and familiar. When a customer hears no—or hears that you've been saying no to other customers—all of a sudden they're more eager to do business with you, willing to wait longer for you and even pay you more. The added benefit for you is the ability to avoid or limit undesirable situations and stave off burnout in the process. There's no career that will ever totally free you from days that feel like drudgery—even dream jobs have those. But the closer you are aligned to work (and customers) you genuinely enjoy, the less it will feel like work, and the more it will feel like a hobby.

BURNED BRIDGES LEAD TO NOWHERE

The end of a partnership needn't turn ugly—
both parties may need each other again

Since the inception of Robert Irvine Foods, one of the more popular items we've offered has been the crab cake. I was always impressed with the flavor we maintained through the freezing and shipping process, and customers were, too.

But as we expanded our product offerings and began to branch into salmon, cod, and more "center of the plate" protein offerings, we needed to find new suppliers. In the grocery business, this complicates things when it comes to servicing your customers—in our case, the Krogers, Sam's Clubs, and Wal-Marts of the world.

Let me explain. Gary Shives, the president of Robert Irvine Foods, visits the various regional buyers, gives a slick presentation showcasing all our offerings, and then the buyers usually tell him they're excited and they want to do a purchase order for X number of each item.

Now that we're working with two suppliers, Gary has to tell them, "Great. That'll be one purchase order for these five items, but we'll have to do a separate one for these crab cakes because they come from another supplier."

At which point he is met with a frown, and we know why. The buyer is now second-guessing, "Do I really want to be doing extra paperwork to get that one additional item? The other five look pretty good . . . maybe I'll just stick with those."

After enough encounters of this nature, we realized we had a problem on our hands. Or maybe not a problem, but an uncomfortable situation. Because that new supplier, it turned out, was capable of making our crab cakes with no dip in quality. So, we call the original crab cake supplier and let them know how things have developed on our end, breaking the news that the long and fruitful relationship we've enjoyed to this point has now run its course. We need to make a change to ensure the continued growth and success of our business. Did they understand? Sure. Was it an uncomfortable conversation? Absolutely. But they had been in business long enough to know that it wasn't personal; we weren't trying to hurt them on purpose. It's just the way business goes.

The most instructive part of that situation is the fact that it didn't end there. After some time with the new supplier, we did, in fact, notice some quality control issues that weren't there in the beginning and had to start shopping for a new supplier—and much to our chagrin, we needed to find individual suppliers for some of the items again. At which point, we placed a call to the original crab cake supplier and asked them if they'd like to get back into business with us.

See how that works?

We were able to make this call because when the business relationship ended the first time, no one had freaked out and acted unprofessionally. They were able to take the call—and the business—and not reject us out of hand due to stubbornness or a desire to give us a taste of our own medicine, because they were experienced enough to never take these moves personally.

Young entrepreneurs—and plenty of unscrupulous experienced ones that I have no desire to do business with anymore—often fail this test. Their energy, enthusiasm, and pride can create a stellar product, but with so much of their self-worth and identity tied up in success, it can prevent them from accepting the fact that temporary roadblocks are just that—temporary. They see any person or thing standing in their way as an affront to their vision—an enemy, an obstacle that needs to be eliminated.

If our original crab cake supplier had felt that way about us, we couldn't have had a second chance.

In my own career I can think of dozens of examples where my view of the bigger picture served me well. Especially in a field as competitive and stressful as TV production, if you're going to take every critical note or rejection as an opportunity to allow some kind of personal vendetta to fester, you're not going to make it very far. In business, if this is your approach you'll almost certainly flame out long before you can ever taste success.

BUSYWORK

Before you can get down to business,
you may have to spin your wheels a bit

One of the things that most people outside of the business world don't have much of a stomach for are meetings. That's OK. There are plenty of people within the business world who hate meetings, too, with yours truly firmly within that camp. And I'll tell you why: meetings suck. They're boring, the small talk rarely feels genuine, and most times they don't yield anything concrete. Even when the meeting could be categorized as productive, you're rarely ever able to draw a straight line back from a product launch or partnership to a specific meeting.

I'm thinking now of Justin calling to tell me that Wal-Mart decided to carry one of our new products nationwide and how he'd react had I responded with, "Thank God we had that meeting with them in New York four years ago!" He'd probably be confused, unable to recall the meeting in question or what its significance was.

Why? Because the intent of a meeting is not to create concrete plans or partnerships on the spot. Their real function is to serve as building blocks in a relationship.

When the CEO of a company takes a meeting with me or one of my lieutenants, they're not always coming in with a specific idea for how I would fit into the fold. They're coming in trying to get clarity on a thought that's been running through their head: *I wonder what this guy's really like.*

That is a perfectly reasonable and valid question. If the "real" Robert Irvine was a far cry from the sentimental guy who gets all weepy with the restaurant owners every Thursday night on TV—say I rolled around with an entourage fifteen-deep, including hangers-on from high school and a guy whose sole job was making sure I never run out of tequila—I wouldn't be an anomaly. I'd be just what they had seen a million times before: another entertainment business phony—seemingly down-to-earth when the cameras are rolling, but an arrogant monster the second they're off. It's a well-worn cliché for good reason, and genuinely surprising when someone happens to stray from it.

When a meeting gets off to a sluggish start with idle chitchat, your likely instinct is to run. But you can't run, so you get right down to business. Hell, you barely have any time to yourself. Why would you want to waste it with some stranger? Just get to the point, amirite? As much logical sense as that makes, getting straight to business can sometimes hurt you. If the other party wants to first kibitz about the weather and the new season of *Yellowstone* and "oh-did-you-see-this-on-the-news," you're screwing up if you try to rush past it and offer only head nods and one-word answers.

Remember: They're trying to feel you out. By the time you got into the room, they already knew what your work is like and the general reputation of you and your company. It's unlikely they have concerns about the quality of what it is you have to offer. Their concern, rather, is: *What will it be like to deal with this person all the time?*

Which, if you remember, is the same question you need to ask yourself when you're making a hire. By the time you've called someone in for an interview, you've seen their résumé and you already know if they're qualified or not. You're now trying to figure out if you can stand their presence on a daily basis, because if you can't, all the talent in the world shouldn't land them the job. That's why we have exploratory meetings. Now's not necessarily the time to talk about the specifics of what the partnership or sales arrangement might look like. The folks on the other side just need to make sure that you'd be a decent person to deal with on the regular. And you should want to know what they're like, too. Sure, they have big reach and could get your product onto a lot of shelves, but are they cold and callous? Wouldn't it be better if you figured that out now before you're in contract for millions of dollars' worth of deliverables?

But for the sake of this example, let's say you go with your first instinct, which is to get down to the brass tacks. After all, characters in movies and TV shows are always saying that and it's always appreciated!

"Someone who gets right down to business. *I like that.*"

Hey, by all means, if you're with a high-level company officer who is blunt and gets right to the point, follow their lead. You don't need to backtrack and say, "Wait! I wanna talk about the Mets first."

But if, as is more often than not the case, they want to talk about this and that, and you reciprocate by acting put out, a great relationship might be destroyed before it ever had a chance to form. Think about it from their end: they gave you a very easy way into a conversation and you brought nothing to the table. Now they've got a bad taste in their mouths before you ever start talking numbers or logistics.

Now go the other way. Imagine what might happen if you come in and suspend your disbelief in the awkward office setting. Say you at least temporarily decide to treat these people like old friends and really give them a lot when answering their offhand questions. You come armed with questions of your own, and you're ready to dig down deep and find common ground.

"You're from Michigan? Oh, cool. My cousin was a Wolverine. Ever get to see a game there? What a place! No? Michigan State fan? Uh-oh! I really put my foot in my mouth! Hahaha."

And on and on and on. And some part of you deep down might feel sick because you don't really care about Michigan and you haven't spoken to the cousin who went there in ten years, but that part of you can keep quiet for now because finding common ground is important. This will all be over in a few minutes—and then you can get down to business.

FOUR

Social Media: A Blessing and a Curse

How to effectively wield the double-edged sword that can make or break your business

The lion's share of any of today's successful marketing and customer relations campaigns happen on social media. Twitter, Instagram, Facebook, Snapchat, YouTube, TikTok, and a small handful of others are the best ways to build your brand and keep customers engaged with it. Social media is also one of the greatest networking tools ever devised. I can't begin to quantify the value that Twitter alone added to my life. While having my own cable show for a number of years has afforded me access to all the "right" people to make connections with, Twitter simply makes it easier—and more fun—to touch base with like-minded people I might never have found otherwise, casually brainstorm about partnerships, and in some cases, actually have those partnerships come to fruition. Gone are the days of digging through layers of publicists and assistants. I can just tweet at you! I've connected with some of the people who have come through to support the Robert Irvine Foundation and our flagship fundraiser, Beats 'N Eats, in just this way.

It's kind of a miracle, isn't it? This technology isn't even a quarter of a century old—and most of the platforms are much younger than that—and it has fundamentally transformed our world. Advertising, networking, recruiting, and direct sales will never look the same. Ditto for news consumption, content sharing, keeping in touch with family, dating, shopping, and so on.

There are, of course, myriad drawbacks to this new landscape, the most glaring of which is that we've collectively lost our ability to decipher real news from fake, fact from rumor, impostors from the genuine article. We've paid a steep price for this, and it's hard to imagine how drastically we've altered the course of our future as a result. I'll leave it to the sociologists and philosophers to sort out the ramifications of those thorny issues and instead focus on what I can add to the conversation. The immutable fact of our new reality is this: social media is here to stay. It will continue to evolve at a breakneck pace, so it would behoove everyone to find a way to live with it in a way that works best for them. While I think periodic breaks (from all screens) are helpful, I'm more of an advocate of responsible, targeted use than I am of abstention. After all, social media has enriched my life and enhanced my ability to do business in a significant way. Anything that brings so many benefits to our lives was bound to bring with it unforeseen complications. The key, then, is to strike a balance that brings more of the positives into your life and business, and fewer of the drawbacks. Here's how I do just that.

THE POWER OF AN AUTHENTIC VOICE

Being real wins—even when it doesn't look pretty

Writers spend years working to find their voice. It's been quite a journey for me over the past fifteen years from my first book to this one, my fifth, plus years of writing monthly columns in various magazines during that period. The process of finding your voice is really just another way of saying that you're getting comfortable in your own skin. In this case, you're opening the door to the whole world to look inside your mind and soul and letting others see what you think and feel. It doesn't matter if your medium is the written word, video, painting, photography, food, architecture, or horticulture—the same principles apply. You need to hone your craft and pour enough of your real self into it, or it simply won't resonate with people. I've found that the more honest you can be, the better your chances are of connecting with, and eliciting a response from, your audience. Ultimately, this isn't a matter for only entrepreneurs to consider, but everyone seeking meaning and connection in their lives.

For our purposes here, I will say that it's to your benefit when you can blur the line between the personal and the business end of things. When your product and your essential self are deeply intertwined, the public ceases to recognize a difference between fandom and what you're selling. Few do this better than Oprah, whose fervent cult of personality makes it easy for her fans to buy whatever she promotes. They don't weigh the pros and cons of a given Oprah-related purchase in the normal way; there's emotion involved, and that does most of the heavy lifting, suspending credulity and doubt. By the time

Oprah is selling it, for her hardcore fans it's not so much a decision to buy as it is an essential act; it's not just a book, a magazine, or a cable channel they're getting, but a connection with the person they love that is maintained through the purchase.

While Oprah occupies her own stratosphere in this regard, there are plenty of examples of people who have successfully leveraged their own popularity into business success. Another great example is Dr. Dre's Beats headphones, which boast annual revenue over $1.5 billion. Others include Jessica Alba's Honest Company fashion label and Martha Stewart's considerable empire that touches so many different things. Then there are a lot of success stories of celebrity-backed products that don't have much relation to what originally made these people popular. I'm thinking here of Dwayne Johnson and George Clooney's forays into the tequila market, Ryan Reynolds with Aviation Gin, and Mark Wahlberg's burger chain. But in all these examples—whether the personality's expertise is leveraged or not—the unifying principle is communication and authenticity. Each person mentioned here is a master communicator who can passionately convey to an audience what's important to them, and in doing so offer their fans another way to connect.

In my own career, *Restaurant: Impossible*—undoubtedly my biggest success on television—continues to be relevant because people get to see the real me. It's never just been about fixing a restaurant, but helping people navigate emotionally challenging territory, repairing damaged relationships, and giving them the confidence to pursue their dreams. The renovations and menu redesigns are popular aspects of the show that are visually interesting, but I have no doubt that its staying power is due in large part to the fact that I found a way to show my authentic self to people while pulling off the transformations. In my case, the product (a reality makeover show) and the person (a handsome fifty-something Brit with a charming accent, no-nonsense attitude, tough-as-nails-on-the-outside-but-soft-as-a-teddy-bear-on-the-inside persona, smoldering good looks, and a physique descended from Mount Olympus . . . did I miss anything?) have become one and the same.

All my companies and products benefit from the fact that the name Robert Irvine is now synonymous with, and cannot easily be extricated from, certain altruistic values. My most loyal fans are aware that a portion of the purchase from every frozen dinner, FitCrunch bar, or bottle of gin goes to benefit the Robert Irvine Foundation and support our veterans and first responders, but for people only casually acquainted with me, the name still carries with it a lot of positive associations, and that's thanks to what we do on the show.

You can take advantage of the same principles. Remember: You are blessed with owning a business in the age of social media—a golden time in history when you can reach anyone on the planet in an instant. Respect that power and cultivate that presence. Your posts should be all at once prolific, helpful, and positive. Each post should also convey what is unique about you and your brand. Bland positivity won't cut it. You can't worry about your idiosyncrasies and humor alienating part of the audience. These are the things that make you real. Besides, there is no approach to any kind of content creation that will safeguard you from criticism or backlash. There will always be someone out there who simply doesn't like you and what you're selling, and they won't need a good reason. It could be your hair, your clothes, or the sound of your voice. And with that being the case, if you're going to lose people the second you open your mouth, you might as well lose them while unapologetically being yourself.

Remember, too, that criticism in general says much more about the person issuing it than the person receiving it. Everyone processes the world through their own set of filters and biases, and we're predisposed to like or dislike certain things before we've even experienced them. You know you've done this. Think about the movie you couldn't wait to see starring your favorite actor that turned out to be crap. Someone else who wasn't a superfan of that actor might call it crap; you, on the other hand, when offering your verbal review to your friends, probably loaded your opinions with as many caveats as criticisms, "Yeah, not a great film overall . . . It definitely dragged, but the cinematography was great and so-and-so's performance was really interesting." That's fine! We all do it. So just remember that fact when people sound off about your business or product; there are some people who will give you the benefit of the doubt, and others who, for whatever reason, you never had a chance of pleasing. It's no different from the fact that you can't be friends with everyone in your school or workplace; you're on a different wavelength. It's not a good or bad thing. It just is.

Counterintuitively, I've learned that with social media, what is specific tends to win out over what is broad, at least in the long run. Yes, an Instagram butt model is going to get a lot more followers than you, but people forge a more meaningful connection with personalities/business leaders/influencers who don't go to great lengths to conform to a perceived ideal, be it conventional beauty standards or classic broadcast-style speech patterns and presentation; any affect that is not authentic to you should be dropped. Your accent, your lazy eye, your old faded baseball cap that you never take off, your hyper kids wandering in and out of the background of your livestream—these are the specific details that will get your audience to see you not just as an "account" they follow but as a real person to whom they can relate. The glimpse they get into the real you builds trust, and once you've built trust with someone, they don't just want to be your customers; they want to become a party to your success. Think about it: Apply too much polish to that vintage wooden end table and . . . congrats, it looks like any other piece of furniture. You just sacrificed the character that made it interesting.

So, now you're putting yourself out there on the regular, sharing in an authentic way, and have built up a nice little following. And by "nice little following," I mean if you can get twenty thousand highly engaged followers who like, comment, and share your posts, that's a number that is in many ways more powerful than being an actor with a million followers. Remember: The actor didn't have to cultivate any kind of online presence or persona to get those followers. People just knew his name so they followed him. And since he doesn't take the time to craft a decent post—rather just spouts announcements about his next project or "It was so great to see Tom for lunch today" (flexing on everyone by making you guess whether he's talking about Hanks or Cruise)—only a very low percentage of his followers really engage with what he has to say.

If I'm being honest, I wish I had learned to use social media in this way earlier in my career. I have a good following these days and you'll notice that I now let it all hang out. I'm a highly prolific Twitter user, which means I don't agonize over typos and at times my vocabulary consists of 50 percent emoji. (Hey, if I text with you, this is what you get, so I give the same to the wider world, too.)

But the top accounts on Instagram, YouTube, and TikTok are not people who were known for something else before they got on social media. They were simply better than most at removing the artificial barrier that always seems to form between us and our audience when the camera is turned on. Brené Brown's book *Daring Greatly* did a fantastic job of pinpointing the source of this power; the most influential social media users are the ones who are truly vulnerable with their content. It's incredibly difficult for most people to be vulnerable and bare their true selves—even to their closest friends and family members—so when they see vulnerability in someone who can do so in front of a large audience, there is an instant respect that transcends the superficial. They take what you have to say a little more seriously and—when the time comes—are a little more eager to open up their wallets.

Positivity

*Customers will respond when you
choose to "shine your light"*

Another unifying factor of the most effective social media users is positivity. They don't get dragged into pointless flame wars, complain about things beyond their control, use their platform to yell at UPS for a lost package, or make caricatures of other people's ideas. Twitter's character limit begs all its users to be as reductive as possible. When you've got 280 letters, punctuation marks, and spaces to make your point, you tend to reach down and grab the strongest words you can find. "I agree with your premise but I think you could make your point in a more constructive manner" is not a tweet that will get a lot of attention. But if you instead define the person you're talking to with an insult that recalls their biggest blunder, then craft a short joke to make a mockery of their position, then that's going to do really well! And since the whole game is getting as big an audience as possible for what you have to say, even well-meaning people tend to fall into this trap.

You see how this double-edged sword is particularly sharp, and if you're posting a lot, you're destined at some point to get sucked into some nonsense or another. It happens, but you can't let it become a habit. The antidote is to be present. Take a deep breath and ask yourself why you're about to write what you want to write. Is it to convey information? Is it out of a genuine desire to help someone? Or is it to win an argument? To get revenge on someone for the mean thing they just said about you? Remember again that the people you want to reach (not to mention future employers, employees, and business partners) are watching how you're interacting with the world. If people appreciate vulnerability, they have an even deeper appreciation for people who can stay above the fray in ways that they sometimes are unable to do. There's tremendous value, as well, in only using social media to disseminate your message. There is no rule that says you have to read the comments or spend any time scrolling through your feed. The easiest way to derail a productive workday is to log on and see what everyone's talking about today. I can pretty much guarantee you it won't be anything that will help you roll out the project you ought to be working on. Drama is the lifeblood of the internet, and mindlessly surfing social channels allows millions of strangers to set your agenda for the day. Don't give into the temptation.

Gordana Biernat—an author/thought leader/influencer we were proud to feature on the cover of *Robert Irvine Magazine*—uses social media only as a means to spread her positive message of love and peace and to help others manifest their biggest dreams. You won't catch her shrieking about current events or politics, sarcastically subtweeting people she doesn't like, or angrily retorting, even when folks get rude. She calls this "shining your light." Her repeated mantra is: *Does this come from a place of love?* She asks herself this question before every important decision and everything she posts. You should also ask yourself this question often. You'll stay your baser instincts not just when it comes to social media but in all areas of your life.

It's OK to Say Nothing

Why you need to be careful when
weighing in on current events

Last, as hard as it might be, resist the urge to chime in on every bit of breaking news. The speed at which a story "develops" on social media is simply too fast to ever be certain that tomorrow you'll be able to stand by what you said today. A complete set of facts, not to mention additional context and perspective, elude even the best of us in the moment. The temptation to chime in is hardwired in our brains: the desire to share both moments of joy and misery is a part of the human condition, the communal experience of discussion serving as a gift during good times, a salve to our wounds in moments of tragedy.

So why hold back here, Robert? Why should I keep silent? Won't people like to see that my business cares? I thought being authentic means being honest with my opinions.

Those are valid points. I'm not saying to hold back out of the fear of potentially alienating a customer on one side or another of the political divide (though that is a reality you need to be aware of). I'm saying that by chiming in before the full facts about any event are revealed, not only could you be contributing to a culture of misinformation; you could screw up so badly that your company becomes synonymous with the blunder.

Here's a hypothetical: Footage from a hotel security camera goes viral. In it, a Domino's Pizza delivery guy shows up to the lobby where he's met by someone who, instead of handing the guy a tip or saying thank you, reels back and slugs the guy in the face, knocking him out. We see him look around, temporarily unsure what to do, then pick up the pizza and run away.

The video instantly trends on Twitter and Facebook and every public figure from Dame Judi Dench to Carrot Top has issued a statement condemning the assault. Every brand from Microsoft to Oreo is using the hashtag #JusticeForDominosGuy. And no one is cleaning up better than Pizza Hut, which, in a deftly clever move, has gone way over the top in an apparent show of solidarity with Domino's, suspending the pizza wars and offering the poor delivery guy and his family free pizza for life. "That's smart!" you say, correctly thinking that the cost of a few pizzas is nothing compared to the global goodwill they've just bought for themselves.

And you'd be right! Except . . . well, the video that went viral didn't have any audio. But thanks to a bystander's smartphone footage that emerges a day later, the full exchange can now be heard. And it goes something like this:

DELIVERY GUY: Hey, man. You seem cool so I wanted to give you a heads-up to stay away from the petting zoo across the street. I just wired the alpaca pen to explode next time it opens. Always hated those things . . .

CUSTOMER: Not on my watch, you sonofabitch.

[WHAM—the customer lands the cleanest knockout punch ever thrown.]

Then the customer picks up the pizza and leaves for the petting zoo, where, we learn later, he defused the bomb while consuming the whole pie. (Bomb disposal is nerve-racking stuff, and apparently burns a ton of calories.)

The whole world is now deleting their previous comments condemning the customer. The most strident reactions also warrant official retractions, apologies, and donations to the customer's charity of choice.

There are no winners in this scenario. Not even our heroic customer, because there will always be some people who only heard about the first half of the story where he looked like a complete monster. The biggest losers? The celebrities and brands who weighed in, cynically trying to capture some of that sweet, sweet viral energy and got burned in the process. They weren't just wrong—they were out of their depth. I repeat: You and your business do not need to weigh in on current events. The official Bubble-Yum Twitter account does not need to exalt or condemn anyone or anything. It should occasionally remind us that Bubble-Yum still exists and stay quiet about absolutely everything else.

The above example is a ridiculous farce, sure, but how many times do we need to get absolutely scorched by out-of-context video footage and other still-developing stories before we learn our lesson? Again, I'm not saying you need to shut up because you might be wrong. I'm saying leave the tough stuff to the authorities and experts and continue to treat your social channels as marketing tools. When something universally tragic happens, such as a natural disaster, it's fine to share condolences. But no one is monitoring your accounts to see where you stand on the matter of earthquake victims. Saying nothing—and remembering to cancel any scheduled posts that you might have had planned through CoSchedule or Hootsuite or a similar program—is always valid.

Now, let's lower the stakes a bit. Let's say a public figure . . .
drumroll . . . said a bad thing. No, their words were not hateful
and they didn't hurt or harass anyone. They just committed the
cardinal sin of publicly expressing an opinion that is not in
vogue at this particular moment. I know, I know. Don't get me
started. The nerve of this person, right?

So you see their name trending and you're curious, and you
can't help yourself and you click on the link to see what this
person said.

*Oh. Hmm. Actually, that is pretty bad. Ugh. Why would they
say such a thing?*

(Well, between you and me, I've had a lunch meeting or two
with that person, and trust me . . . the thing they stupidly said in
public is a *mild* version of what they're really thinking.)

But that's neither here nor there at the moment. What matters is that you've had a visceral reaction to the bad thing that
was said and you've got thoughts about it and you feel like
giving them a piece of your mind. Let the whole world know
where you stand on the bad thing. Good idea, right? For you
and your brand to be publicly aligned against the bad thing?

Nope. Don't take this the wrong way, but I swear on my life
that no one cares what you or your brand think about the bad
thing. If people are following you, it's to learn more about you
and your brand. So even though some of your louder, more passionate followers might come out and ask you directly what you
think of the bad thing, you're under no obligation to answer, as
easy as doing so might seem.

But Robert, if it's so easy to answer, why wouldn't I just do it?

Because there's a hidden cost to answering. In the short term,
you'll get the too-online crazies off your back for condemning
the obviously bad thing. And it's not like your less-engaged

followers who didn't care one way or another what you thought about the bad thing will be annoyed by your answer—but the moment you choose to chime in on internet bullshit, you are no longer unsullied. You've now gotten down into the muck, and you are no longer an oasis for people who can't stand the muck and the way we're forced to breathe it every day and let it seep into our pores. Don't give in to the temptation. If you sell chocolate candy, keep selling chocolate candy. Post about how great chocolate is and where it came from and how you make yours and isn't it so great and don't you want some right now? This isn't burying your head in the sand. Rather, this is, as Gordana would call it, "shining your light." This is refusing to get pulled into senseless drama. This makes a statement of its own: that you're an adult and you don't need to be part of an elementary school–style pile-on to be a righteous human being.

Remember: You're here on this planet because you were called to be great at something. Keep being great at that something. It's why people like you, follow you, and maybe even love you and what you bring to this life. The kinds of things that may cause public uproar are constantly shifting. Something that someone said publicly without incident just five years ago could be cause for a massive firestorm today. Staying focused on what matters—and more specifically, what brings more joy into people's lives—is a virtue that, I promise, will never go out of style.

EMBRACING TECHNOLOGY

The future is coming, regardless of how ready you are

Social media is just one way in which technology is changing our world and the way we do business. I had some thoughts on the bigger picture of how tech is shaping our lives—in particular how businesses must deal with the breathtaking pace of change itself—in a keynote speech I delivered in 2019 to the nSight tech conference hosted by nCino, a cloud banking service. A lightly edited version of that speech is presented here.

Change Is Constant

In every phase of my life, I've seen firsthand the incredible good fortune that awaits individuals, organizations, and businesses who embrace change. Because the truth is, change is the only constant. Like it or not, the only thing we're really guaranteed is the fact that the world will not slow down no matter how much we might like it to.

Likewise, I've seen firsthand the misfortune that befalls those who try to resist change. Who try to stay fixed in the same exact way of doing things forever. We can get tricked into thinking that we're preserving a tradition or a way of life by resisting change—especially new technology. But that's a fallacy. We're perfectly capable of honoring the traditions of our forebears without living exactly as they did. We can have a Thanksgiving dinner without hunting for the turkey, cleaning it, and roasting it over a fire.

So, when you meet someone who says they're more "old-fashioned" and who seems intimidated by something like cloud banking, remind them of this. Remind them that technology doesn't kill traditions. If anything, we can use technology to enhance a tradition.

As you've witnessed throughout this conference, banking technology is advancing at warp speed. But as good as nCino wants to make this technology, and as much as that tech makes things easier for bankers and their customers, people won't want it unless they can walk into one of your branches and get that warm smile and handshake—which is of course the way it's always been. That tradition of a caring human being who's watching over the shop will never go out of style—even if all the systems around that human being are in a constant state of flux.

I'm not a banker and I don't write software. Nevertheless, I'm here because I've had a lot of life experience that is relevant to what you're talking about.

I'm a veteran of the British Royal Navy. I'm also a veteran of the restaurant industry. Both enterprises have undergone sweeping, radical change just in my lifetime. The basic function of these institutions hasn't changed a bit. Militaries fight. Restaurants feed people. The mission is the same. But how we accomplish those missions is always changing, and that's due in large part to technology.

If you or people within your organization are resistant to change, be kind to yourselves and to them. Because it's natural to be a little bit scared of change. Change requires courage and we're not hardwired to seek change. We're hardwired to seek comfort. It took us how many thousands of years to get to this point where we can binge-watch any show we want and not get off the couch all day? And have Taco Bell delivered? I mean, come on! From an evolutionary standpoint of avoiding risk—which is paramount if you're just talking about survival and staying safe from predators—there has never, ever been a better time to be alive.

Of course, these comfort zones feel wonderful, but as has been said of them: nothing ever grows there. Our attachment to our comfort zones is killing us physically—look no further than the worldwide obesity epidemic. And comfort zones can kill businesses, too. I know why it happens because I know how long it can take to get a business to a place where it finally runs smoothly. You build and build and build for years and then, once things are finally going good, you get a chance to put it on autopilot.

That's what many business leaders do and it's a huge mistake. It's dangerous to check out because what usually follows is they stop trying to get better. They stop trying to make things easier, faster, and more enjoyable for the customer because they don't feel like it's necessary any longer.

Well, guess what? In the restaurant business and in banking, if you're not always in the process of making things better, easier, and faster for your customers all the time—if you take your foot off the gas—there's another restaurant and another bank down the street, where they're working their tails off to make things very attractive for your customers.

Simply put, if you don't pay attention and stay ahead, they're not going to be your customers anymore. And then you're going to be out of business. Because failure to innovate is the business equivalent of watching Netflix and eating takeout all day.

Technological Change in the Military

Militaries, throughout history, have never been organizations that need to be coached into embracing new technology. Because in their case we're not talking about dollars and cents—we're talking about life and death. No general ever said, "Call me old-fashioned, but I don't want the latest weapons technology. We're not going to use that surveillance drone, we'll just send a thousand men over the hill. They'll never be able to shoot them all."

It's a stark example because in the military, the survival of their "business" quite literally means the survival of their people and the way of life they're fighting to protect.

I left the military in the 1990s. Where they are now versus then in terms of technology is a thousand times more advanced. We're not flying over targets anymore; we're firing laser-guided missiles from many miles away. And by the way, we don't have to fly people anywhere if we don't want to. We have unmanned drones patrolling the highways in Iraq and Afghanistan and the pilots are sitting at a control panel in an office building in New Mexico drinking coffee.

Better and more advanced as it pertains to the military means they're not just more lethal but considerably more efficient. Frigates that previously needed 240 men to operate now require only 100. And we don't need as many ships. What we have is smaller, nimbler, and can get where it's needed faster.

In the British Royal Navy, Her Majesty's Naval Base Devonport—better known as Plymouth Dockyard in England—is facing massive cuts. At one point in history it was the pride of my homeland, harbor to the most feared naval force in the world. Now its role is considered far less crucial.

There's been a lot of waxing poetic about it, and I understand that all too well. It's sad for me to say goodbye to some of these things from the old world, things I grew up with, things that were fixed in my mind as constants. But my life and career path have taught me that these moments are necessary.

Change is evolution, a necessary part of life. But change can also be painful. That's OK. Sometimes you have to feel that pain and go with it anyway. Be scared, but dive in.

If you folks in the financial services industry could see into the future and see what the competition was developing and the kinds of experiences they were prepared to offer their customers, then you might think a bit more like our Joint Chiefs of Staff and you might be a little more aggressive about pursuing new technology. It would behoove all of you to think in the same terms as our military: pursuing new technology isn't merely a matter of profitability but a matter of survival.

Technology in *Restaurant: Impossible*

In the restaurant industry, stubbornness has killed more businesses than are in operation today. I know because on *Restaurant: Impossible*, we've visited hundreds of them and still haven't come close to visiting all the owners who wrote to us and asked for help.

In all those hundreds of establishments, I've encountered filthy kitchens, drab décor, rotten or non-existent business plans, rude waitstaffs, and owners who completely lacked leadership—not to mention some really terrible food.

I've also encountered a small handful of places that had a good handle on certain elements of running a successful restaurant; some had a good menu but the service was terrible, some had an attractive dining room and a good gimmick but the kitchen was too inconsistent to generate steady business.

But in all of them—no matter what problem they had—one of the unifying factors behind their issues was stubbornness. Behind every failing restaurant was an owner who—even though they had called me in to help!—protested changes I wanted to make. They would say some variation of "Oh, well, you can't tell me to change my tomato sauce, that's an old family recipe."

The most extreme example I've ever encountered was Paul's Bowling in Paterson, New Jersey. The bar-slash-bowling alley had a long history in the area, and some loyal patrons, but it had a lot of problems owing to the fact that the owner was a true technophobe. He didn't own a computer. He didn't know how to text or send email. His point-of-sale system was beyond dated. It was an old cash register with a bell.

And in the bowling lanes, he had pencil-and-paper score-cards. I get that there are some old-timers who might appreciate this, but if you want new customers—particularly young people with disposable income—come on. People will come visit you for rustic charm. But they don't want to hang out in a mausoleum.

We did the renovation and it certainly looked a lot nicer. The menu was cleaned up and we installed iPads for scorecards to replace paper and pencil, but the real work on that episode was trying to train a man—who had never used a smartphone—on how to send a text message. Think about that and how much harder it was for him to get in touch with staff and make simple shift changes. A mass text message or email couldn't be sent. He'd have to call each person individually. We helped him with that, and in the short run I know we gave the place a fighting chance. We checked in with them after a few months and after a few years, and things were up a lot from where they had been.

But the real X-factor is the owner's commitment to change. Is he going to stay up on it? Will he continue with upkeep and will he continue to learn? Or will he consider the makeover the end of his journey? I can only set him up and point him in the right direction. I can't run his day-to-day or instill a value of self-improvement. And if he's still afraid of new things and technology, there's only so far the changes I made will take him.

When I'm not on TV, I'm running several of my own businesses. I've been around. People don't allow me to walk into their restaurants, tear the place apart, rebuild it, and change the menu in two days just because I know how to cook. I'm a businessman. And I don't make decisions based on emotion. I make decisions based on math.

The balance sheet doesn't lie to you. People will. Customers, colleagues, partners, and vendors will all lie if they feel like they have to. It doesn't have to be malicious in intent. A lot of times when people lie they're trying to shield you from something unpleasant. That's in our nature. Yes, you need to surround yourself with people you can trust and depend on, but always remember that numbers are the only thing that never lie.

I learned a lot of this, of course, by doing it. I've had plenty of business ventures that didn't work in the exact way I wanted—be it a restaurant or a TV show or a food product—things that, even though I was passionate about them, I had to ditch when I saw the numbers. You can love a product all you want, but if the customers don't love it, too, it's time to move on.

A great example of this in my own business life is Robert Irvine Foods. We're only seven years old, but we've changed our offerings considerably over that time based on the numbers. We're proud of everything we've ever put on store shelves, but the reality in this business is some things hit and some don't. And if a product doesn't catch on quickly, you've got to move on just as quickly and not be sentimental about it.

Then there are times when maybe you've got something popular—a hit that people really seem to enjoy—but the numbers still aren't making sense. For example, when we started, Fit Crust Pizza was a big item for us. People liked it and we sold a good amount of it. But the competition in frozen pizza is so tight that it's very hard to make enough money for it to be worth the time and effort required.

Meaning: Between production and shipping and keeping our prices competitive with the other leading brands, we were profitable, but not profitable enough to justify the amount of staff we had dedicated to the product. After a certain point, you have to say, "Would the bottom line be better served if we were offering something different? If we took all the resources we're using to make pizza and redeploy them in a smarter way?"

In this case, we did just that. We spent time to R&D new products and moved from things like pizza and side dishes right to the protein in the center of the plate. Chicken, fish, pork, beef. We learned that if you do these things right you can sell them for more, at a higher profit, with a larger margin for error because the competition can't do what we do in those areas.

With that example in hand, look to your own product portfolio and be honest. What products and services are you still offering to consumers out of a sense of tradition or continuity rather than from a pure profitability standpoint?

Another key point you should know: When it comes to my restaurants, Fresh Kitchen by Robert Irvine in the Pentagon and Robert Irvine's Public House at the Tropicana in Las Vegas, new technology has been a massive boon to us. A few years ago, I decided to embrace new restaurant management software that takes the guesswork out of running a restaurant.

Everything on the staffing side, from hiring, to scheduling, to the log book, to payroll, to accounting—all of it runs through the software. It's a huge time-saver, and of course, time is money in any business.

In the kitchen—and this is where it gets really interesting— the software provides some incredible inventory management tools. This makes it much easier to track rotation, which simply means that the first items we put in the fridge and cupboard are the first items we use. This not only cuts down on waste—which is a moral issue—but increases profitability.

The system also alerts us to when we need to order more of a certain item, because the software knows that for each chicken sandwich we sell, we're using x amount of lettuce, x amount of breadcrumbs, x tablespoons of mayonnaise, x teaspoons of salt and pepper, and on and on and on. So every time a server goes to a workstation to order food from the kitchen, the system is logging everything and keeping track. You're not just getting data on what your most popular items are at certain times of day; you stay on top of your inventory down to the ounce and teaspoon.

When I started out in the culinary profession almost thirty years ago, if you had told me that technology like this would exist and allow you to automate the thankless, nitty-gritty aspects of running a restaurant, I would have thought it was science fiction. But it's not far off in the future. It's here now and it runs better than I ever could have imagined.

Yes, there's a lot of work involved in setting it up and training your staff how to use it properly, but once you do, it gives the whole business a fail-safe. If you have this technology and still screw up your inventory, you only have human factors to blame. It's not because you didn't have the means to stay organized.

On the consumer-facing side of things, we've made it a point of emphasis to have servers speak to diners as they receive each course.

How is everything? Are you enjoying it? Then, at the end of the meal, *Anything you think we could do better next time?*

We've learned that by doing this immediately, we're able to quell any potential bad feelings before they fester and become serious issues. Because, yes, customers speak up if they get the wrong order, and they usually speak up if they're very dissatisfied with the way something is cooked, but nine times out of ten, if they simply find the experience mediocre and have no plans to return . . . well, they're not going to say anything; meanwhile, on the ride home they're logging on to Yelp and letting you have it with a two-star review. "The fries were soggy. Service was slow. My wine glass had lipstick on it." And so on.

Sending surveys to customers via email or text is another great way to get this information.

If we give customers an opportunity to tell us what they really think—in person or via a survey—we have found that most of the time, even a very dissatisfied customer will not take their gripes public to Yelp or Google Reviews or Twitter or Facebook. They'll feel that the need they had to express themselves is now satisfied and the urge to lash out is dissipated. It also puts the feedback data directly into the hands of the business where it can do some good, rather than floating around out there on the internet where it can only hurt the establishment.

I cannot begin to tell you how valuable this is as the restaurant industry has been totally transformed by Yelp and it takes a tremendous amount of hard work to negate bad online reviews. Because what's the other phenomenon at play here? Some people will log on to give you a good review, but you have to *really* knock the socks off the average person to get them to take the time to do that. On the other hand, if they're pissed that they spent money on a bad experience, they need no encouragement to fling some mud at you. They're going to do it. But if you give people an open forum where they can sound off, we often stop that before it happens.

Remember: Not all publicity is good publicity.

Self-Reflection

It might seem counterintuitive to do this when all we're talking about is forward-thinking and embracing new technology, but something else that you'll want to do is look to your past. What products and services need to be dusted off and resurrected? And if you were to bring them back, how could they benefit from new technology that wasn't there on the first go-round?

Nostalgia is a powerful force. We all yearn for the return of the old familiar thing that's been given new life. Look no further than the reboots and sequels that dominate the current entertainment landscape.

I've benefited from this phenomenon myself. After shooting fourteen seasons of *Restaurant: Impossible*, we wrapped up in the spring of 2016. Food Network looked at the numbers and the ratings were not where they had been in the show's heyday, so they chose not to renew it. I didn't disagree. The show had a wonderful run. It helped a lot of people. It entertained a lot of people. But all good things must come to an end, right? That includes *Seinfeld*, *M*A*S*H*, and *Restaurant: Impossible*.

But a funny thing happened over the next three years: the fans wouldn't let the show die. They kept asking me and Food Network to bring it back. Every. Single. Day. And once Food Network was sold from Scripps to Discovery, we revisited the idea and decided to test the waters with a mini-order of four new episodes.

As we approached it, we said, "Let's not just pick up where we left off and make more episodes. Let's make it even better. Let's improve the video quality and camera work and editing. Let's put the focus on the emotional heart of this show, which is, of course, not the restaurant itself—not a building—but the people behind it. Let's put the focus on what they're fighting for and why it's important to them." Then, with a slightly tweaked approach to production that didn't lose what made the show so popular in the first place, we set out to deliver what the people had been asking for.

So, how'd it go?

Well, the overnight ratings were a smash—nearly two million viewers on a Saturday night on cable—straight into the Top Ten for the night, and Food Network immediately ordered and fast-tracked more episodes so that we could make a proper season out of this. It's humbling and very gratifying to be in this spot—especially when I had thought for so long that the show was behind me—but it is nevertheless a testament to the power of nostalgia, to the value in listening to your customers and giving them what they want, and to the fact that sometimes the key to the future might be in your past.

And did the show's return benefit from new technology? You bet it did. The quality of a shoulder-mounted camera rig—just in the three years the show was off the air—improved to such a huge degree that every frame of the show looks better no matter what you're watching it on. The colors are brighter, the images more crisp and detailed. People's TVs also got a lot better in that time, too, and were able to take advantage of all the detail we were capturing.

Whether you pride yourself on being on that bleeding edge or you take a more cautious wait-and-see approach, there's never a bad time to embrace new technology. It's never too late to take advantage of something that's always in the process of getting better.

For an example specific to just your industry, let me ask you: Did ATMs replace banks?

Of course not. It made banks more efficient. It freed up bankers to concentrate on bigger, more important tasks than simple but time-consuming things like small cash withdrawals and deposits and balance inquiries.

So how do you get ahead of what's next? I wish I could tell you about some new and exciting technology that only a few people know about that will make you rich beyond your wildest dreams. But I'm not a fortune-teller. I've just become disciplined when it comes to listening to people who are experts in their respective fields. I give almost total autonomy to my various department heads and I listen to them when they have a great idea. You've got a pitch that could make my life easier? I want to hear it.

But in the end, remember: Technology, in and of itself, is merely a tool. Employ it properly and it will help you accomplish your mission. But technology can't give you your mission. It can't give you leadership skills, instincts, or a passion for what you do. You still have to provide that. And for that fact, we should all be grateful.

The American inventor Dean Kamen—creator of a revolutionary wheelchair called the iBOT—said, "Every once in a while, a new technology, an old problem, and a big idea turn into an innovation."

That statement is a brilliant one; part of what it means is that the human element is crucial. Without smart, passionate people dedicated to using all this technology to solve real problems for real people, it doesn't accomplish anything. Without *you*, it's just a shiny new electric guitar with no musician to play it; a state-of-the-art kitchen with no chefs to cook in it; a 4K movie camera without a cinematographer to capture the scene.

We're not in some sci-fi dystopia. Technology still works for us. It won't replace what you do—it will make you better at what you do. Embracing it is a way of investing in yourself and the continued development of your business.

It's also another way of showing faith in the fact that you and your people are irreplaceable. Great talent always is.

FIVE

Is It All about Money?

Know what your partners want before you start signing papers

Nobody is in business to lose money or just break even. We all need money, and healthy businesses make money. But the underlying motivating factors need to be carefully considered when you're choosing business partners. While it might be true that everyone wants to make money, it's not true that money is the end-all goal for everyone. For some, their business is their legacy and they want it to positively impact their customers, employees, and community. For these folks—and I count myself among them—money is a tool to enhance and expand the business's mission of service.

People from either camp might create a successful business, but when a businessperson from the school of "money is everything" partners with a businessperson from the school of altruism, it's a good bet that rocky waters are ahead. In good times, the money-focused business partner will want to take dividends out of the profits, and the altruistic partner will want to take the profits and reinvest in the company. In bad times, the money-focused partner will want to keep their salary and benefits exactly where they are and look at other ways of reducing costs—from shedding payroll to cutting corners on product quality. The altruistic partner, meanwhile, takes a more humane approach to their employees and is more willing to make personal sacrifices. This disparity in philosophy is enough to sink the business.

David Jeffries, my contracts attorney, sits business partners down with one another and runs through hypothetical scenarios to take their temperature on these important issues. He also insists that partners clearly delineate areas of responsibility. When you're small and just starting out, it's easy for both parties to roll up their sleeves and just do what needs to be done. But success and growth complicate things, and a failure to outline who is charge of what can halt that growth.

And when you're outlining who's in charge of what, this needs to be more than a verbal agreement. Get it in writing. Dave makes this part of all his contracts, and his clients always thank him for it later.

"This process almost always yields areas that had been overlooked," he says. "Almost every time, they recognize things they hadn't been thinking about. I understand why it gets overlooked. In the initial phases, everyone is so excited and working so hard that they're focused on how exciting it all is. But eventually, someone needs to be paying attention to the nitty-gritty stuff, the stuff that isn't so fun, and if you don't have it clearly outlined who needs to do that, you're in for a lot of heartache."

Romantic partners who start restaurants are in for a particularly rude awakening. The combination that I typically see on

Restaurant: Impossible is that one is the chef, the other the brains who makes all the financial decisions. But communication breakdowns are serious and common even in marriages that don't double as business partnerships. When you factor in the long hours required to run a restaurant, the difficulty increases exponentially. For one thing, working together doesn't make couples closer; with one spouse in the kitchen and the other in the office, they might as well be on different planets. See the introductory case study of Joe Willy's Fish Shack; when you pepper in financial struggles, the relationship stress becomes unbelievable, enough to break any marriage.

This scenario is easily extrapolated into other relationships. No, you might not be married to your current business partner, but it's not unusual for partnerships to evolve out of close friendships. Think hard about that relationship and what it will undergo as your lives and finances become further enmeshed in the partnership and how that other person responds to stress and difficulty. Is the friendship strong enough to withstand hardship? How will you feel if you lose that friendship? Conversely, look in the mirror and be honest: Are you prone to playing the blame game when mistakes are made? Or are you comfortable taking ownership and making amends?

And last: Does your partner strengthen you and bring out the best in you? Do they have a work ethic and passion that is infectious and inspires you to go beyond what you thought you were capable of? Or do they rely on you for inspiration and motivation? And if so, are you strong enough to provide that as your own workload increases?

Honest answers to all these questions can determine the fate of your business—and alter the course of your life.

The Country Cow/
Covered Bridge Farm Table

The Country Cow in Campton, New Hampshire, had a unique problem. Co-owners Kerry Benton and Jenny Leonzi were divorced. They had met while working together at another restaurant, dated for a couple of years, married, then opened the Country Cow ten days after tying the knot. The stress of running the business immediately spilled over into their marriage, which ended after sixteen months. But with their finances firmly entwined—and debt mounting—their business partnership, fraught as it was, endured.

From initial sales of $900,000 in the first year, that number fell by more than half as Kerry's anger problems ran downhill to the rest of the staff; whenever something wasn't right, he threw pots and pans and berated employees for not living up to his standard. Meanwhile, that standard was lousy. During my initial visit in 2014, customers complained about long wait times and the uninspired food they were served.

Naturally, Jenny was on the receiving end of a lot of Kerry's abuse. While working with Kerry, I came to understand that his anger issues likely had their root in his relationship with his father, who rode him hard and pushed him for perfection. In a terribly emotional scene where we cleaned out the restaurant to start renovations, Kerry grabbed a few of his father's vintage toys and wept openly, revealing that his need for money was so dire that a few years prior he had worked instead of attending his father's funeral.

I felt terrible for Kerry, but also for the rest of the staff, which was forced to absorb the result of these unresolved issues. "Some people have drugs or alcohol. I have anger," Kerry said. At the end of Day 1, I told him to go home that night and think hard. Did he really want to make the restaurant work or did he want out? Early the next day, Jenny and I got some shocking news. Kerry indeed wanted out. He signed over everything to Jenny on the spot and walked away.

Both parties felt that an enormous weight had lifted. I then took Jenny down to the river and asked her to let it all out. She threw rocks into the water, and with each stone she cast, she said goodbye to something terrible Kerry had called her during their lowest moments.

Armed with a newly remodeled restaurant and re-vamped menu, Jenny took the reins and charged ahead. So how did it go? I went to find out in an episode of *Restaurant: Impossible Revisited* in 2019. Five years had passed, but Jenny's beautiful restaurant still looked pretty much brand new. It also had a new name. It was no longer the Country Cow, but the Covered Bridge Farm Table, which highlighted the restaurant's calling card—a beautiful view of the adjacent river and covered bridge, which I loved. It wasn't just Jenny putting her own spin on things or removing the last vestiges of the original partnership that created the restaurant; it was the perfect business decision.

Moreover, Jenny had no kitchen experience when I first met her, and had since taken a twelve-week crash course in culinary training and had further redesigned the menu to give diners a unique experience they couldn't get anywhere else in the area. In that show's big moment, she told me that annual sales when I had visited were just shy of half a million dollars, and had since climbed to over $1.2 million.

The packed house service I observed was seamless and customers appeared delighted to be there. Most importantly, Jenny was totally invigorated and so was the staff, setting the Covered Bridge Farm Table up for success for many years to come.

There's a valuable lesson here for anyone who can't stand their business partner—or their domestic partner. It might not be impossible to work through your problems—you already know I don't believe in the word "impossible"—but if that relationship is so toxic that it's poisoning everything it touches, there's no valor in sticking it out. Kerry had cited his main reason for hanging on as a fear of legal liability; he felt if he walked away and saddled Jenny with the debt, he could be sued and the restaurant would continue to haunt him for years to come. He figured it was better to try to fix it. The main reason Jenny had cited was a desire to stick to the original plan. "We came into this together, we're going to get out of this together," she said.

They were both clinging to a sunk cost fallacy, and it made me wonder how many people out there stay in bad situations for reasons that simply don't add up. You must be honest with yourself about what you want and what you need. If your business or business partnerships aren't serving those wants and needs, ask why you're still hanging on. If it's to avoid some sense that walking away equals failure or a waste of time, I've got news for you: that feeling is temporary, and it's nothing compared to the feeling of letting years or decades go by before it finally blows up in your face.

To Kerry's credit, he realized this and finally walked away. To Jenny's credit, she realized she could build a new life out of the ashes of the old one.

In the most surprising reveal of the revisit, Jenny told me that after leaving, Kerry had since helped her cater events and even visited the Covered Bridge Farm Table to have dinner with his new girlfriend.

In the end, everyone got what they needed by having the strength to let go of their old notions of what success was supposed to look like. Remember: This journey is oftentimes very challenging, but it's not supposed to be miserable.

MONEY AND FAMILY: THE MIX THAT NEVER WORKS

Accepting investments from the people closest to you is more fraught than you probably realize

In the beginning, you may have nothing but the product. No facility. No team. No distribution or marketing models.

But hey, you can figure all that stuff out at some point down the road. All that matters right now is that this product is a winner and you know it. And when the world can finally get their hands on it, they'll know it, too. Your passion and commitment to your idea is strong enough to overcome any obstacle in your path.

Be that as it may, without some money to get started, your great idea remains just that—a hypothetical worldwide phenomenon that will stubbornly remain a secret until you can get hold of enough capital. So, in your hurry to get started, you start looking around at those closest to you. Your brothers and sisters, aunts and uncles, cousins and close friends—maybe they'd want to finance your early operations for a stake in the company. And unlike a bank, they don't require collateral or a mountain of paperwork.

Great idea, right? Not so much. This kind of ad hoc family financing fails more often than it succeeds. There are lots of reasons for this, starting with the fact that if this is your first rodeo, you're likely underestimating the amount of capital necessary to get under way. When it's your second, third, or fourth product or business launch, you have a much better sense of the unexpected hidden costs that are bound to crop up.

Things like . . . Your prototype fails. Your logo looks too much like an existing logo and needs to be redesigned lest you get sued for trademark infringement. In the case of a restaurant, maybe the paint job you chose for the dining room looked great in the showroom, but when paired with the cozy romantic lighting you have, it makes your dining room look like a haunted house. There are myriad tiny disasters that will visit you on the way to launch. And every little delay—even the ones that don't cost very much—takes time to fix. This has a more insidious secondary effect because the delay itself has a steep cost; every moment that you're repairing something is a moment you aren't bringing in money.

Proper lenders and experienced business partners who deal with this every day will anticipate these setbacks. And besides offering the financial backing to float you through the rough patch, they can offer advice, solutions, and other resources to help. Your friends and family? There isn't much they can offer you here but headaches. Even assuming they're fully supportive and aren't frustrated by a lack of progress, if you do have to ask for more money, it can strain the relationship. They might give it out of a sense of obligation, but you can see how this might easily be a turd in the punch bowl at Christmas. So let me underscore the point: using your family to raise capital is a high-wire act that invites disaster. It is hard enough to start a successful business. Great ideas fail every day. Even in boom times, there's a lot at risk. Your familial relationships should not be part of that risk.

What's more, each time you bring on an investor, you're relinquishing a percentage of your company. It's a hard hole to dig out of if you've already auctioned off 30 percent of your business before you've made a single dollar. You might think you're fine because you've still got 70 percent, but that ignores the fact that there is always further dilution that happens down the line as you need to raise additional capital. You need to stay comfortably above 50 percent ownership so you can stay in control of all major decisions and day-to-day operations. Yes, bigger investors will get special voting rights on major moves you want to make, but staying above 50 percent ensures that you have the biggest say in the fate of your business. Find proper lenders and business partners. It might be more work to find people and situations you feel you can trust. But if, in the end, you lose your business, you won't be losing your family, too.

David Jeffries was my teacher for a lot of this. He counseled me against bad deals and negotiating away too much of a stake in my own companies, and he was a steadying voice whenever things got rocky. He had operated within the business world for long enough that he knew nothing moves in a straight line. The path to success is a crooked, sometimes messy, zigzagging path. It's a step forward, then a step back, then to one side, then to the other, and then forward. Through him, I came to realize that the unpredictability was normal and nothing to panic over. In fact, when I first got into business with him, one of the first things he did was help end my involvement in Robert Irvine's Eat!, my restaurant in Hilton Head, South Carolina.

Initially, I had been thrilled to open the restaurant, and like so many other new restaurants, it started out with a bang. We had a good concept and a great staff. But the name on the marquee—yours truly—spent almost all his time on the road filming. At that point in my career, I had yet to collect a core group of chefs to support my vision and operations. So we had a lot of great line cooks, but with my not being there every day or at least a few days a week to keep a close eye on things, it was only a matter of time before quality started to slip and public interest waned. The lesson for me wasn't that I couldn't own a restaurant as long as I was pursuing a TV career; it was that I needed to surround myself with more talented people that I trusted at the very highest level.

Today, I have that in place with four key hires. I have an incredibly talented executive chef, Brian Goodman, and corporate chef, Tito Marino, to assist me on the set of *Restaurant: Impossible*. They run planning for all my events: from serving thousands at one of Gary Sinise's Invincible Spirit Festivals to support the troops, to regional food and wine festivals.

Ensuring that my restaurants run smoothly while maintaining peak quality is VP of culinary affairs Darryl Moiles. Currently, Darryl splits his time between Robert Irvine's Public

House in Las Vegas and Fresh Kitchen by Robert Irvine in the Pentagon. I hired Darryl away from the Four Seasons in Boston and it was one of the smartest decisions I ever made. Darryl isn't just a remarkably talented chef; he's a born leader and a stickler for details.

Last, and most certainly not least, is Shane Cash, who's been on my team longer than anyone else. I met Shane back in the 1990s when we were both working at the Trump Taj Mahal. Today, as VP of product development, Shane's day-to-day job is testing and creating new products to roll out for Robert Irvine Foods.

Together, these four are the beating heart of so much of what we do. They work together seamlessly and support each other without ego. And when necessary, they're all so talented that they can each step up to fill in for one another. When I'm cooking for a huge crowd—like for over five thousand at the Airpower Foundation's Annual Skyball veterans benefit—it's the combined effort of these four that makes it possible.

To take it back to my earlier point about how success is a jagged path, I had to make a couple of hires that weren't the best fit until I was able to assemble this dream team. And to make hires of the Shane-Darryl-Brian-Tito caliber, I had to set my ego aside because they're just so incredibly talented. I wouldn't want to go up against any of them in a *Chopped-* or *Iron Chef*-style competition, and it's safe to say that a younger Robert might not have been comfortable enough in his own skin to make these hires.

But now that I'm older and wiser, I can see that the best and biggest companies don't get to where they are because they have a super CEO at the top who's the best at doing everything. Business is a team sport and the CEO is the head coach. He needs to understand psychology and how to best motivate each player to get the most out of everyone. The end goal is to win, not to win and get all the credit. In short, I'm past the stage of my career where I want to be the Michael Jordan of everything. I'm perfectly happy to be Phil Jackson. In the end, we're all getting championship rings, right?

THE IMPORTANCE OF GIVING BACK

Philanthropy isn't just a moral value—
it's good for business

The Robert Irvine Foundation is the driving force behind everything I do. The story of its creation, though, goes beyond a personal desire to help our veterans. The RIF fulfills not just a deep personal need—but also a broader need of corporate responsibility. I believe it is incumbent upon all companies that do well to give back to the communities where they are based. Yes, you pay your local, state, and federal taxes. And yes, you paid your town for the easements needed to make your establishment bigger or more attractive to customers. But you're not done yet. The moment you move beyond making a living to turning a profit, you need to look beyond your doors and think of how you can give back.

I'm a capitalist and always have been. For the most part I think the government is big enough, and unwieldy at that. Energetic individuals and companies working in the private sector can almost always do a better and faster job of getting things done than elected officials who are engaged in an endless pitched battle with the slow-turning gears of bureaucracy.

But if that's true—and most businesspeople I know would agree with at least the general premise of the sentiment—then we need to step up and do something for the communities that have done so much for us. If your company is profitable and you don't like it when someone suggests we need more government programs, well then, Mr. Private Sector, shouldn't you be stepping in?

It doesn't need to be a massive commitment. For me and my companies, what we're able to give back has always been a question of scale; the bigger we get, the more we're able to give. Hence, in our current configuration with food, liquor, and protein companies all contributing to the Robert Irvine Foundation, we're able to do quite a bit from paying for improvements to homeless veteran shelters, serving thousands of troops and their families at various festivals, touring with the USO, helping to build specially adapted homes for disabled veterans, and donating powered wheelchairs and other gear to wounded veterans in need.

Nothing makes me prouder than our current capabilities, and as long as there is breath in my lungs, I will continue doing everything I can to increase those capabilities so we can have an even bigger impact on the veteran community.

You're probably not yet asking yourself how to grow your own foundation for maximum impact, and that's fine. But surely your luncheonette/widget factory/bike repair shop is doing well enough to sponsor a little league team, donate to the local food bank, pay for an underprivileged kid's trip to summer camp, or buy dinner and drinks for the local VFW now and then. Giving back is a broad mandate and it can mean a lot of different things to different people. You don't have to give till it hurts, but give you must. As with so much other advice I've given in this book, again I will say that if you can't do it for the right reasons, do it for the fact that it further entrenches your brand as a part of your community, which, of course, is good for business.

Smith's Soul Food Bistro

Good intentions can't run a business. Just ask Cheryl Littlejohn. A former NCAA champion with the Tennessee Lady Vols basketball team and a former college coach, Littlejohn opened Smith's Soul Food Bistro with the idea that it would employ at-risk youths in the underserved area of Gastonia, North Carolina. On that level, Smith's was a success; the teenage servers I met were delightful and enthusiastic, with Littlejohn giving them an opportunity to save money and learn the value of hard work and how to set goals.

On every other level, though, Smith's was a failure. In its eleven-month history, it did little besides hemorrhage money. Small wonder. It served soul food as bland as its dining room, which was about as cozy as the DMV. When I observed a service, my eyes were opened to one of the biggest problems: the head chef Keith didn't have a recipe book. He had a list of ingredients that didn't even contain measurements. To illustrate how absurd this was, I put all the ingredients for chocolate mousse in front of him and said have at it. Without measurements or a process to work with, he wound up handing me a brown soup that tasted like coffee.

Yet I understood his reasoning for the not-quite-a-recipe book: *he* could remember what he was supposed to do when he saw his ingredient list, so why bother writing it all out? OK, but what happens when he's out sick or on vacation? Or what happens to the dish that's ordered a bit less frequently than the others and isn't as well-practiced as all the others? Consistency is a difficult thing to master even under the best conditions. When you're flying by the seat of your pants every day the way Keith was? You've got no chance.

Cheryl, meanwhile, wasn't even using her coaching skills. In a basketball gym, she had been a master of delegation and instruction. Here in the restaurant, where she was much less sure of herself, she resorted to micromanaging. "I see it as protecting my investment," she argued.

I wanted to yell, "Hey, Coach! You ever go into a game without a game plan?! No?! Then why are you doing a different job every day? And why doesn't your chef even measure his ingredients?" It made me mad, except . . . I couldn't stay mad at Cheryl. Not when her cause was this noble and there were so many bright young kids depending on the success of Smith's Soul Food Bistro to give them a better shot in life.

In our heart-to-heart I learned she had been fired from her college coaching job for a variety of NCAA rules violations, chief among them being she had given undisclosed gifts to recruits. Lost in the "rule breaker" narrative that chased Cheryl out of coaching was the fact that the clothes and money she gifted were to students in need. She had broken rules, sure, but her heart was in the right place.

I decided that I needed to reconnect Cheryl with her coaching roots. We went outside to a basketball court and I had her coach her servers through a pick-and-roll play. It had been many years since Cheryl had done it, but I wouldn't have known that by watching. She gave clear, concise instructions. She was energized and perfectly authoritative. She was in such perfect command of the situation, no one dared interrupt; their attention was rapt.

I saw the smile on her face and couldn't help but smile, too. And without another word from me, Cheryl knew what she needed to do: get back in the restaurant, make a playbook, and coach. Keith needed precise recipes, but he also needed to be empowered to run the kitchen without someone questioning every decision. Deborah Currence—Cheryl's sister and business partner who had a background in finance—would need to take full control of Smith's finances. No more micromanaging. Coaches, after all, can't play the game for their players. The whole job is putting them in a position to succeed.

In a highly emotional address shortly before the restaurant reopened, Cheryl gave the pregame speech of a lifetime that fired up everyone, including me.

"We've got more than soul food on our menu," she said. "We've got empowerment on our menu. We've got inspiration on our menu. We are not going to allow the past to dictate our future."

She then made a series of promises, and at the top of the list was "No more shortcuts."

Shortcuts, after all, had not just driven Smith's to the brink of bankruptcy; they had torpedoed Cheryl's coaching career. Yes, she had acted with good intentions, but there was an aboveboard way of helping the kids she wanted to help that would have left her coaching career intact. To hear her allude to this with her promise of ditching shortcuts for good was one of the most encouraging signs I've ever seen from an owner. I didn't need to push her in that direction and draw the parallel; she did that all on her own. She knew she needed to change. The new menu and remodel helped reinforce that desire to change. Remember: It's hard to feel you're just doing business as usual when everything that surrounds you is brand new.

It was a successful trip to Gastonia, and not just because sales went up 34 percent after I left. It was successful because those teenage servers who had been given a second chance now had renewed faith in the security of their own futures.

One fifteen-year-old server, Alazjha, told me, "Cheryl taught me that I was appreciated." Alazjha had had a tough childhood, and feeling appreciated by a powerful figure like Cheryl had made all the difference in the world.

Now imagine for a moment what Alazjha and all the other servers might go on to achieve, and who they might inspire, who they might give chances to, who they might affect. This isn't about one person, but every other life that person touches. The knock-on effect is exponentially bigger than any of us could realize, because one good act can ripple far beyond what we can see.

It gives me goose bumps to think about it, and I hope you take it to heart and understand how important this lesson is. In whatever way you can, big or small, I implore you to use your business to give back to the community it serves. In order to do that, of course, you'll need to keep the business healthy. Good intentions can only get you so far. Meaningful impacts and outcomes are created when your intentions are met with concrete actions.

PART 2

Overcoming Impossible in Your Mindset

SIX

Know Your Why

Or you're destined for mediocrity

Often lost amid the minutiae of how to build a business is *why* you want to build a business. What are the reasons behind your actions? Are you just doing it for the money? The notoriety? Or are you genuinely attempting to add value to people's lives? The reason you're doing something can mean the difference between being happy and fulfilled throughout the process or totally miserable. Eventually, it will also mean the difference between success and failure.

People often chase making it big in business—and seeing their names on placards, products, and billboards—because they are looking for external validation. They think that if they collect enough stuff "out there," it can assuage all doubts and fears that live within the mind. Even if you forget for a moment that nothing external can ever truly satisfy you, the fact remains that work done for cynical and greedy reasons is usually destined to fail.

Why? Because today's consumers are pretty good at spotting fakes. They turn up their nose at crappy merchandise, but also at silly ideas, phony marketing campaigns, and the cynical people behind them. You needn't call to mind every cheap product you ever bought that fell apart after a few days to offer me a counterpoint. I know there's plenty of lousy merchandise out there and plenty of people who unwittingly buy it every day. My point is that the companies and business leaders who really last are almost always the ones standing behind a quality product that adds value to people's lives.

And so, we come back to the why. Starting a business requires time, energy, and expertise, but the driver behind all those factors is passion. You need to step back and ask yourself some serious questions and give yourself the space to answer honestly. Ask yourself if this is something you truly believe in. Then ask whether this a project you would still want to pursue if money and fame were not motivating factors. Last and most important: What benefit can I give to the world by making this successful? Am I providing something that people truly want and need? Does it give back to my community, my country, my world in a meaningful way? An element of service above self can go a long way in keeping you engaged with your work on a deeper level and making you want to see it succeed beyond reasons of your own bottom line. When you have that final element behind your product, you create loyalty, and a legion of customers who will want it to succeed as badly as you do, people who give you the most coveted form of marketing that can't be bought: positive word of mouth.

It's just a matter of zeroing in on what you're passionate about. In my case, I identified my why early on. I loved cooking because of the instant gratification it gave me: You put a hot plate of delicious food in front of people and you get to see them smile. You see their day get brighter and you can bask in the positive vibes and great conversation that come from that. Great food really can bring people together.

Beyond that, I loved to help people and see their lives transformed. Hence, you can see how my career evolved into *Restaurant: Impossible*, which is the ultimate distillation and combination of my two greatest passions—cooking and helping people. The staying power of *Restaurant: Impossible* is due in large part to the fact that there's real passion behind it. Yes, the show is a good idea on paper, but shows don't exceed three hundred episodes over the course of twenty-two seasons on the strength of marketing alone. There needs to be a real fire at the heart of something like that, and I'm incredibly proud to have lit it.

Yet I wanted to do more. I wanted to leave a bigger impact and help even more people than just the families whose restaurants we saved each week on TV—a desire that led me to create the Robert Irvine Foundation, which I wrote about earlier.

I'm endlessly fascinated and grateful that my career has worked out the way that it did—in a way that I never could have imagined when I was starting out. It began with a focus on my passions that then combined in practically perfect, serendipitous ways.

The lesson here is to stay focused on what excites you. Don't get distracted by what other people are doing or trick yourself into thinking you need to follow their path. Your passion and work ethic—if they are great enough—can forge brand-new paths where only wilderness had existed before. If I had articulated a desire to combine my disparate passions back when I was starting out in the 1990s, I wouldn't have been able to convince many people that it was viable. After all, what analogue did I have for what I wanted? I couldn't point to anyone else who had been able to pull it off on the scale I had intended.

But here's another secret: I didn't bother telling anyone. I kept my grandest desires and ambitions to myself. I instinctively knew that every moment I spent trying to convince others of my ultimate potential was a moment that I wasn't spending on actually getting there.

As a society, it's a lesson that many of us haven't learned. "Fake it till you make it" is the mantra of the social media age. Hundreds, if not thousands, of "CEOs" litter LinkedIn, make-believe bigshots in charge of one-person companies with no capital, no plan, and no future. Don't be tempted to make a show of success before you get there. It can feel empowering in the moment, but it's ultimately fool's gold that pulls you off course from what needs to be done—and in a few pages I'm going to share a powerful cautionary tale of putting the cart before the horse.

KNOW YOUR WHY
RESTAURANT: IMPOSSIBLE CASE STUDY

From Across the Pond

I could have chosen more than half of the episodes of *Restaurant: Impossible* for a good example of this principle at work, but I settled on one from recent memory, the premiere of Season 20: "Extreme British Makeover." In this episode, I visited From Across the Pond in Colleyville,

Texas, to find owner Dan Herdman, another British expat, who had fallen on exceptionally hard times. Through two failed restaurants, Herdman had squandered his life savings of over $400,000. The financial stress eventually proved too great for his marriage, which failed, as well. By the time I visited, he was a broken man, feeling he had failed to provide for his two sons and his second wife, co-owner Jodie Sellers. In his darkest moments, he contemplated suicide several times. Hanging on by a thread, he worked in the kitchen to try to help things along. But he had little culinary experience and the food he served up in his gluten-free British pub was pretty average and way too greasy. Because most menu items ran through the deep fryer, wait times were atrocious. What's more, the place looked nothing like the British pubs I loved, devoid of the character and cozy atmosphere that make them such comfortable places to sit for a meal or a proper drinking session.

The place needed a thorough overhaul, and of course we gave it that. But the central issue was Dan. His eyes were sunken. He slouched. He talked about himself like he was a loser. No menu revamp or remodel could have helped long-term unless Dan started believing in his ability as an owner and a leader. He needed to stand tall in the front of the house and oversee operations, not run around lost in the kitchen. To get him to a better place, we had to do a lot of work. First, I asked him to write about all his failures and read them aloud to me, which he did through tears with his wife beside him. I then asked him to put all those pages in a metal trash bin and set them on fire. "That's all behind you," I told him. "The only thing ahead now is the future." Next, I took him outside to play a game of football (soccer to you Yanks) with his staff. He was loose. He was free. He cracked a smile.

Finally, he was ready to remember his *why*. Why he had started such an oddly specific restaurant—a *gluten-free* British pub in the heart of Texas. Indeed, why had he? Turned out it was for his son, who has celiac disease. He wanted a place where his son and other people with the same affliction could enjoy all the comforts of his home-land. With a solid enough menu, the gluten-free aspect would draw everyone in through the doors, not just people with celiac disease or those trying to avoid gluten to lose weight.

Today, he's on his way to that dream, with sales up 40 percent since I left town, and he's even hired two new chefs to execute his vision. Whether he stays on course and rebuilds his nest egg is another story yet to be told, but he can get there. He just needs to keep standing tall, stay away from the negative self-talk, and keep his why in the forefront of his mind.

FIND WHAT YOU'RE BEST AT

What's trending might seem sexier,
but it'll blow up in your face if you don't love it

I've told plenty of people to follow their passions, but I also know the phrase has become a cliché, co-opted by an endless supply of internet-era self-help gurus. You may have seen it so many times it ceases to hold meaning, or you dismiss it as new-age pablum. Fair enough. So let's rework this sentiment to instead say: find what you're best at. For an example in this passage, we'll say that the thing you're best at is making French toast. But French toast is old-fashioned, and as you sit down and put your thinking cap on, you realize that because it's not trendy, people don't seem to be willing to pay a premium for it like another simple food, such as avocado toast. So now you're tempted: since avocado toast is the hotter item at the moment, you should make that. Maybe you could work on developing a dozen varieties and sell them from a specialty food truck that becomes all the rage in a young, hip city.

Now you really start to think big. After all, this is a daydream rooted in a market reality: People want this stuff! They pay way above cost for it! You could make a killing. You might sell out every day and expand to a fleet of trucks that cover the whole city. The more you think about it, the more it sounds like the perfect idea. All you can see are dollar signs.

Oh, but you forgot one very important thing, didn't you? French toast is what you love and you don't really give a shit about avocado toast. Yeah, it's good. Fine. Whatever. You could take it or leave it. But that doesn't matter, you tell yourself, because you can make it and market it and the business is there.

But in deciding to chase a trend and toss your passion—or what you're best at—by the wayside, you've limited your endeavor from the get-go. You must accept it as true that if you do not *love* what you are doing, there is little chance that others will. We often can't explain why we love things. We just *do*. Somehow, we are just hardwired to more fully appreciate the way a particular thing looks, sounds, tastes, and, especially, makes us *feel*. And that's the key. The thing that naturally moves you is the thing that you need to build your future around, because true love—not infatuation or temporary excitement—never dies. The reasons why you love it don't diminish, they grow, and you find new things to appreciate about it. Like a successful marriage of many years, you are in a constant state of rediscovering one another, finding that extra layer that gives you something new to love.

So. Back to that French toast you make so well. No, there aren't any trending news stories about it, and the younger generation isn't waiting around the block for it. But have they had yours? What if you fully committed to it? And continued perfecting and evolving your recipe and process and developing new varieties? What if you decided for yourself that you were going to make the best damn French toast in the world because that's what *you* want to eat, market trends be damned?

What would happen then? Who knows. Success, of course, isn't guaranteed just because you do what you're best at. But of this I am certain: it gives you your very best chance to succeed. Chasing ever-shifting, elusive trends that you can't predict or control, on the other hand, is all but guaranteed to turn your dreams into dust.

WHAT YOU'RE BEST AT
RESTAURANT: IMPOSSIBLE CASE STUDY

Turnpike's Rest Stop

Turnpike's Rest Stop in Springfield, Florida, provided an abject lesson in the perils of ignoring what you're best at.

Eric and Jodi Parresol founded and owned Turnpike, and the signature item was oversized sub sandwiches. How oversized? When I came in to watch a service, I was aghast; some of these things had enough meat and cheese to feed a family of four. Fifteen customers left with two dozen takeout containers. I had to laugh. Then I tried them. Not great, not terrible, as a Soviet nuclear physicist might say. But I couldn't get my mouth around these things, and I had to keep wondering who even wanted to eat stuff like this. It was a borderline obscene amount of food.

I didn't need to look at the books to know that food costs had to be out of control and that the owners needed to work from a totally different concept.

I went in the kitchen and met the head chef and general manager, Melissa Parresol, daughter of the two owners. A trained pastry chef with nearly two decades of professional kitchen experience, she knew what she was doing and ran things efficiently. But she had a scowl on her face as she worked. She wasn't in love with giant sandwiches and it showed on the plate.

Here was a head chef in the unenviable position of executing a menu she never wanted anything to do with, and she felt it wasn't her place to step up and say the restaurant's founding concept was a disaster.

Bizarrely, during the course of that episode, no one ever did articulate exactly why they had ever thought it was a good idea to serve someone almost two pounds of pastrami on a roll. But I had my suspicions. Everyone in business wants to be known for a thing. The temptation to go huge and give people the impression of serious value was too much for the Parresols to pass up. It's not impossible to make such a concept work—just ask half the delis in Manhattan. But I guarantee you those delis are priced appropriately and do enough volume to make it work. Rent alone means you have to serve a ton of customers in New York if you want to stay in business.

So I took Melissa outside, away from her parents. We sat down and I asked her: If you could make Turnpike's into anything you want, what would it be? What are *you* best at? A woman after my own heart, she said she'd serve breakfast, specifically upscale Southern grandma style. The next day she came in and served me and her parents a brisket and pancetta dish with fried eggs. It was outrageously good. I added a few menu items of my own: strawberry cheesecake French toast, steak and eggs, and a duck confit hash, and they were off to the races.

We also transformed the restaurant from a dark, muddled collection of kitsch and license plates to something simpler, cleaner, more modern, with an industrial feel to pay homage to Eric's first career as an auto mechanic. The space now reflects something meaningful to the owners, and the menu reflects something meaningful to Melissa.

As I watched Melissa get to work on her new menu on Day 2, I couldn't stop smiling. I was happy because she was happy, and her enthusiasm for the task was infectious. It spread to her parents and the staff. Her parents have since brought Melissa on as a co-owner, and that enthusiasm has spread to the customers; revenue is up 35 percent.

The lesson is so simple, but business leaders forget it all the time: Give talented, creative people an outlet to express their authentic selves and bring creativity into their work and the investment will pay you back. Chase a trend—or a random gimmick that you hope turns into a calling card—and you're all but doomed to fail.

Counterpoint

Even great products that creators love can fail

In 2016, I developed what I thought was going to be a slam-dunk product: the flat chicken. Essentially, this was a spatchcock chicken, butterflied so it lies flat with the breast bone removed. It's a great technique that reduces cooking time and allows the meat to roast evenly and lie low in the pan so that every portion cooks in its own juices, creating a finished product that's moist and tender. The knife skills required to remove the ribs and breastbone are not particularly advanced, but they are also not part of the repertoire of most home cooks, so my thinking was clear: if we did this prep work for the consumer—and developed a killer rub to package it in—then we could have ordinary families eating whole, delicious roast chicken any night of the week by putting in the same amount of effort it takes to cook a frozen pizza.

Working alongside Shane Cash, who heads R&D for Robert Irvine Foods, we were certain we had nailed it. It didn't take much testing or tinkering—we quickly landed on something that made my mouth water, something that I'd be proud to serve up in my restaurants but would be available in stores everywhere. It was an exciting time!

I cut a few promo videos and we fired up the social media marketing machine, getting the word out to as many people as we could that they just had to try this amazing new product.

And yet, just a few months after its release, I had to pull the item due to flagging sales.

So what the hell happened? It certainly wasn't a lack of passion or know-how. I was making what I was best at. Anyone who knows me knows that one of my favorite dinners is whole roast chicken. My heart was all the way in on this one, and it was Good with a capital *G*.

The long answer involves some rollout issues with our retail partners whose employees didn't know whether to freeze or refrigerate the product, leading to a heartbreaking amount of spoilage. The short answer is that the consumers were confused, too. My product might have been great, but no one knew what the hell I was selling. It wasn't a raw, whole chicken they were used to seeing in the meat section and it wasn't a fully cooked rotisserie chicken they could just bring home and eat from the package.

Spatchcock chicken is something that not nearly enough people are familiar with to actively seek out and buy. They might try it in a restaurant but when they're pushing a shopping cart around with a screaming toddler in the front, they're not going to branch too far out of their comfort zones as they check off their shopping lists. If Robert Irvine Foods had perhaps launched a thirty-minute infomercial about the product, or run cooking demos in every major grocery chain, then maybe it could have caught on, though turning a profit would have been a steep uphill battle with that kind of marketing budget. When you don't have that kind of mass-education campaign around a product launch and such a wide gulf exists between your product and public awareness of what category it's even in, then you're in trouble. It's hard enough to make something great that can be replicated and maintain quality on a large scale. If you need to add consumer education to your rollout, then the game is probably over before it even begins.

Failing, of course, is never comfortable. All your work and research is geared toward success, and when it doesn't work out the way you intended, it's upsetting. But I've learned to give myself room to fail because, as I wrote in the introduction, there really is no better teacher. It's fine to fail, but it's also incumbent on you to learn the right lessons so you don't fail the same way twice.

If all I had learned from the flat chicken experience was that people didn't want spatchcock chicken or know enough about it, then the core problem would repeat itself. Yes, those details about public awareness around spatchcock chicken are true, but what was the bigger picture? You need to take the specific lesson and extrapolate it to learn a larger truth about the business you're in. In this case, I learned that I needed to work closer to existing categories and that there is usually too much heavy lifting involved with creating a brand-new one.

SELF-AWARENESS

Why having a firm grasp on how others see you is crucial

Take your work seriously, but never yourself. Within this distinction is the core of who I am. After my family, I live and breathe for my work, my businesses, and my employees. I take what we do as seriously as brain surgeons need to take their work. For better or worse, my career has always received the full measure of my focus and energy.

But over the years, I have learned to walk the tightrope of being fully invested in the work while removing the essence of who I am from the outcome. In short: I am not my work.

I don't need to be deferred to, called "sir," or shown any special treatment by anyone. Not from my right-hand man Justin, not from the on-set intern who takes the lunch order. When I screw up, I can laugh. Others can laugh. In fact, I've found there's no better way to maintain perspective and refocus on the task at hand.

Picture this: It's late at night and we just finished filming an episode of *Restaurant: Impossible*. The crew is packing up the equipment and cleaning up our mess. Then there's me, entering hour sixteen of the workday, hunched over a laptop, watching footage of a different episode set to air in a few days and providing voiceover work.

I see the line I'm supposed to read right in front of me, but there isn't enough—or possibly too much?—caffeine in my system to make my tongue do what I need it to. I'm exhausted and all I want to do is get back to my hotel room and face-plant on the bed. But no one's going anywhere until I get it right.

Just read the damn line, Robert. You can read, can't you?

If I'm being honest, I didn't love the copy. Too many clauses and unnatural pauses. In a perfect world, we'd sit down and do a rewrite and simplify the whole thing, but that would require time we just didn't have. And so the tension mounted, higher and higher with each flub, reset, and fresh take.

I couldn't take it anymore. I pushed myself back from the table, gave myself a few gentle slaps to the face, hit the deck, and started doing push-ups. I then stood up and did a few jumping jacks. The bleary-eyed crew didn't know what the hell was going on.

I stopped for a moment to address them. "The blood clearly isn't getting to my brain!" I laughed. "I know I look like an idiot, but if anyone cares to join me so I'm not alone, you're more than welcome!"

The crew laughed and exchanged a few glances and shrugs. Then, at midnight in an empty restaurant dining room, seven people who had been on their feet for way too long and could barely stand up straight worked out for five minutes, chiding each other for sloppy form and laughing the whole time.

Minutes later, back at the laptop-and-microphone setup, I didn't nail the line on the first try, but I did on the second, and we finished the whole recording shortly thereafter.

That moment to break the tension and remind myself that I'm human was essential for me. But in reflecting on that moment in the years since, I've realized that it was essential for my employees, too. They are all well-accomplished in their own right. The producers, especially executive producer Jill Littman, the amazing camera crew, the gaffers, the grips, the assistants . . . these are professionals—grown adults with careers, families, and responsibilities that exist whether they continue to work for me or not. And yet . . . I'm cognizant of the fact that if I, the face of the show, had not chosen to make a joke of that moment and instead decided to throw a tantrum and berate the producer who had written the copy I didn't like, the power dynamics of that situation would have dictated that no one could stand up and tell me to cool off or have a laugh about it. They probably would have internalized it, tiptoed through the very uncomfortable ensuing hour, and taken it home with them.

Of course, this happens every day in TV and film. I'm thankful that in the wake of the #MeToo movement, the industry has begun to open up about toxic, corrosive behavior from people in power—behavior that isn't criminal, per se, but nevertheless creates a harrowing experience for everyone in their orbit. This kind of crap is a far cry from going extinct, but slowly more and more people in power are realizing they can't act like children when things don't go their way.

It should be noted that it doesn't take an office-wrecking tantrum to make the people who work under you feel unnecessarily uncomfortable. I would have been well within my rights to grumble, spread a bit of blame, and angrily slog my way through the voiceover. Whoever wrote that copy sure would think twice next time, wouldn't they?

That path, however, is bullshit, pure and simple. The people who work for me are human. They're always doing their best. And the fact is the copy that I could barely read for whatever reason might have flowed easily on another day when I wasn't so damned tired. So if I'm willing to give myself leeway to be a flawed human, don't my employees deserve the same? Doesn't everyone deserve that?

And this is what I mean by having enough self-awareness to not take yourself seriously. In the above example, I was taking the work deadly seriously, especially given the late hour. I wanted nothing more than to nail it perfectly. But if I were someone who also took himself seriously, the embarrassment of flubbing the line over and over would have sent me into a shame spiral that saw me lashing out at other people. Even though such an outburst would have been out of character for me, I could still feel the mounting tension around me. I instinctively sought to break it by making an even bigger fool of myself and turning the whole situation into a joke.

My employees didn't just appreciate the choice. It turned out to be the catalyst that got us the hell out of there and off to bed—not to mention made us closer as the years progressed.

Using that story as a guide, honestly answer these questions: Do you take yourself seriously? How do you feel when you screw up in front of your employees? Embarrassment is natural. It's OK to feel that way. It's not OK to take that negative energy and turn it on other people. In the long run, it destabilizes your business by eroding trust and increasing turnover, not to mention tarnishing your reputation. Oh yeah, people talk! If you can't control yourself for the right reasons, fine—be cynical, and at least do it out of your own self-interest.

SELF-AWARENESS
RESTAURANT: IMPOSSIBLE CASE STUDY

Mr. B's Restaurant

"Aloof" is often synonymous with "harmless," a personality trait that's almost endearing. *Oh, it's almost cute, isn't it? The way he has no clue what's going on around him?*

Well, in some instances, maybe. For a leader, being aloof and lacking self-awareness can be the death sentence of the business.

Take Calvin Jefferson and Ninkia Green, the brother-and-sister pair who took over Mr. B's, their parents' restaurant in Tampa, Florida. At almost half a million dollars in debt, Mr. B's suffered from a lot of typical *Restaurant: Impossible* issues—lousy food, glacial service, and a depressing dining room. All fixable with my usual approach. I wasn't worried about that. I was deeply concerned, however, that the relationship at the heart of this restaurant was stressed to the point of breaking and Calvin didn't even know it.

A full-time pastor at the church across the street, Calvin popped into the restaurant as much as he could to handle big-picture tasks like hiring, training, and, most significantly, promoting the restaurant—conducting interviews with local media and making social media posts in which he encouraged townsfolk to come into *his* restaurant. That's right; in all this running around to drum up business, Calvin left his sister completely out of the story. An egregious oversight to commit against a close family member, never mind one who shouldered the lion's share of the workload to open, close, and run the kitchen.

When I pinpointed this as the central issue that was sinking Mr. B's, I sat the two of them down and told Ninkia to let it all out. "I'm your only sister, but you don't make me feel like that," she told him. "I don't think you have any idea how I leave here every day. You left me out there to do all the work. Either you work with me and help or just let me go, because I can't do this anymore."

Calvin was shocked, replying, "I didn't know I made this kind of a difference in your life."

I then spoke with Calvin alone and asked him to showcase his skills as a minister for me. His main job, after all, was reaching people, touching their hearts, and keeping them engaged with their faith. He needed to do that for Ninkia. His assignment: write a eulogy for his sister. It sounds morbid on its face, but it's really not. It always struck me as odd that we wait until someone we love is gone to then stand in a church or funeral parlor to say what was really in our hearts all these years. It's a salve to the people who have experienced the loss, but for the person who would benefit most from hearing these words, it's too late.

He obliged, telling Ninkia the next day that he always saw her as his "superwoman," a "caretaker," and that he would always be her biggest fan. Through this lens, I could see that Calvin's attempts at running a solo PR campaign for the restaurant weren't a vanity project, but a misguided attempt to help a business partner who already had too much on her plate. If he neglected the relationship, it was only because he put too much stock in his sister's strength.

They cried and embraced, and Calvin told Ninkia, "It's not about me. It's about us." By the end of the episode, they were cutting social media videos together for *our restaurant*, which no longer resembled the depressing bore I had stumbled into. Ninkia didn't just forgive her brother—she proved eminently coachable in the kitchen, where she took a few new dishes and ran with them. Our end title cards revealed a sales increase of 150 percent and the fact that Ninkia had given her first solo interview to local media about the kitchen she proudly ran.

The lesson is simple: self-awareness is essential for every business leader. You need to have a clear and accurate picture of how you're perceived. Don't assume your partners and lieutenants are happy with the way you're running things. You've got to take their temperature and listen to their input. And if you work with family—or people who you grow so close to that they become like a second family—don't dare wait until it's too late to tell them how you really feel.

KEEP IT TO YOURSELF

Why publicly forecasting big success is a dangerous game

Earlier I wrote that I keep my grandest ambitions to myself so I'm not distracted from actually achieving them. Here's another thing that can wait: your big announcement.

Ooooh, boy! Here we go! Big things coming! Had a great meeting today and lemme just say I can't wait to share it with y'all!

I constantly see tweets like this from young professionals and I cringe every time. They have one promising meeting and they're bursting at the seams to tell the whole world that big things are happening and just you wait 'cause it's gonna be a blockbuster.

You needn't reach out and touch this particular hot stove to know to keep your distance. I didn't. I just watched someone else. In the dark ages before the internet—and the infinite opportunities it provides for all of us to embarrass ourselves—a chef friend of mine could not stop running around telling everyone who would listen that he was all set to go to New Zealand within a few months. There was a fancy new resort being built on the coast, and the restaurant would provide the most picturesque ocean views you could ever imagine. So every day, he'd go off about all the new things he was going to do, how he was going to blow the socks off every guest who came through, and how this place—which would initially and obviously be known for its sweeping views—would soon become better known for its food and the bold, creative chef who was set to rewrite the rule book on how to run such a place.

So the days, weeks, and months go by in just this fashion. The big day is coming and as it comes, the chatter from this chef becomes louder and more excited. "You won't see me around here no more! You'll have to come visit paradise! Just be sure to drop my name when you book a room!"

Being totally honest, I wouldn't say I was jealous, but it made me rethink what I was doing at that time, which wasn't anything groundbreaking and was certainly less flashy than what this guy was about to embark upon. Where was my adventure and risk? Why wasn't I doing something cool like that, something that would really make people talk?

Well, the big day finally came. The day when this guy was supposed to be getting on a plane to go start his new life as the magical chef-king of Middle Earth. Only instead of getting on a plane to start designing his menu and dining room, he got a call from the principal investors of the resort. The deal was dead. The permits and leasing agreements had become a massive headache for these guys—who, surprise, surprise, weren't that experienced themselves—so they folded. No shame in that. Happens all the time in business. You pick up, move on, and find a better place for your grand schemes.

As for the chef, however, this was a really tough spot. Much tougher than it needed to be, because you couldn't even categorize this as a failure. The situation was completely beyond his control. But now he was in the awkward position of explaining to all those people he had told for months and months that he was going to the other side of the world to build his little empire why he was still kicking around town and still stuck in his old job. It would have been a bitter disappointment for him regardless, but by constantly running his mouth he compounded that disappointment into public embarrassment. For as many months as he had made his grand plans public, he spent twice as many explaining why they had fallen through. And every time he had to do this, I could see the pain it caused him, with each little conversation about the situation twisting that knife a little more, never allowing the wound to close.

To say I felt bad for the guy is an understatement. I empathized deeply with him because if I had gotten into a similar situation at that point in my career, I probably would have done the same exact thing. *Hell yeah, Robert! Ya hit it big, now go tell the world!* I shuddered at the thought, shook my head, and vowed I'd never fall into the same trap.

There are, however, more reasons to avoid big, public announcements before every last detail is nailed down. Chief among them being the fact that all the energy you spend telling people what you're doing can be spent in any number of more productive ways, doing things that will actually serve your big endeavor if it does indeed go through.

In the case of the chef, he could have taken out a pen and paper and sketched out what he wanted his dining room to look like, began researching ingredient sourcing and designing a menu that incorporated local flavors, or started practicing making those new dishes and perfecting them. Some of that work would have eventually been for naught, of course, but the experience of doing it could have made him a better chef, and his practice planning would have made him that much better prepared to hit the ground running for the next such opportunity that came along. Hopping on social media to craft a look-at-me post, on the other hand, doesn't make you better at anything except absorbing attention. Worse, it can make you addicted to that attention, and it can quickly become a rabbit hole where you spend half a day responding to comments and basking in the make-believe glory of it all. Each comment of support and congratulations, while temporarily gratifying, ratchets up the risk factor, and makes the potential embarrassment loom that much larger.

You can't protect yourself from all embarrassment. There will always be factors outside your control and you may yet feel the pain of falling on your face in a very public way. What I'm urging you to do is avoid self-inflicted wounds, especially those brought on by vanity or amateurish overexcitement. Always say less than is necessary about your plans, and unless they're absolutely imminent, avoid saying anything publicly at all. The moment you begin trying to convince other people about how great your new thing is going to be, you've put your energy "out there" when the magnitude of your task demands that it be "in here."

But wait a second, Robert, I've seen you say stuff like this on Twitter before!

Yes, I have indeed tweeted things like "Big things coming! Can't wait to share more with you!," but I can guarantee you every time I did that I was either in a manufacturing facility and watching actual product come off the assembly line and get stacked onto pallets, or had just finished filming a bunch of episodes of a show that Food Network loved and had already slotted into the next quarter; it just wasn't time to rev up the marketing machine yet, so I kept it vague.

Trust me, there will be time to celebrate. When you work your ass off on that big thing and it finally comes together, you will get your moment to bask. But having gone through it a bunch of times, I can assure you such a day will not be your crowning achievement. Because if you're doing it right, the work itself is the reward, not what everyone else is saying about it. To put it as simply as I can, when you get up in the morning and find true joy in what you do, that is the very definition of success. Once you can get to that place, you won't need to look very far for validation; you will find it in your heart.

SEVEN

Managing Ego

*How unchecked egos will ruin your business—
and how to curb them for good*

I f all you knew about the restaurant industry was what you saw
on *Restaurant: Impossible,* you would probably think that only
control freaks, narcissists, the petulantly stubborn, and the in-
tractably arrogant open restaurants. Considering what I typically go up against, this isn't an unreasonable conclusion to
reach. When I first started making the show, I knew the restaurant industry would be a target-rich environment—one in which
I would never run out of owners who were doing it wrong—but
by the time I finished filming Season 1, I worried that we were
showing too many of the same flaws. How many times could
viewers see a stubborn owner who said everything was fine
when it clearly wasn't?

*Isn't this the same problem they had last week? If the owner
wasn't going to listen, why the hell would they call up* Restaurant:
Impossible? *And where is Robert finding all these delusional people who serve bland, greasy crud in their filthy restaurants?*

In the brief hiatus between seasons, I was in the gym one morning when a thought occurred to me—where such thoughts often occur to me—while I was getting my time in on the elliptical. I had been mentally going through Season 1, thinking of all the problems I had encountered. By this point I had concluded that stubbornness was the unifying factor despite whatever the specific problem of an establishment might be.

So what makes a person stubborn? I asked myself.

My first thought was age. Over time, we simply get stuck in our ways, right? Made sense as it went through my head. But then I went back over the different owners I had encountered. Sure, a few of them were getting on in years, but there were plenty of young owners, too, and they were just as stubborn as the old ones.

Must be pride, then.

OK, but if your restaurant is going out of business, why would you have pride in that? Besides, grime-coated stoves and fridges and rude servers aren't exactly the kinds of things proud people would tend to tolerate. I get that your grandma's recipes being the inspiration for your restaurant might have been a point of pride at some stage, but as the business sinks further and further into the red, that pride would be long gone.

Then it hit me.

Ego.

All the people I had helped had become stubborn and insisted on repeating the same old ideas that didn't work . . . because of ego. We tend to use "ego" or "egotistical" as synonyms for "arrogance," but I'm using "ego" in the primary definition of the word. Yes, ego has come to mean a certain kind of self-importance, but before that it originally meant the part of the self that does the thinking, deciding, and interacting with the outside world.

So if someone thought of an idea—some business or product—that was all their own and it wasn't working, then their inner self-defense mechanisms would immediately kick into over-drive. Problem is, our primitive self-defense instincts don't ask us to calm down and look inward at what we could be doing differently. They instead heighten the situation and stimulate our fight-or-flight reflexes. That's why so many of these stubborn owners also lash out at their employees and family members. It's not unusual for dissatisfied customers who speak up and complain to get an earful, as well.

So, we've got business owners with bruised egos who are making life hell for everyone around them, all while clinging to bad ideas that aren't working, and hemorrhaging money every step of the way.

The show to that point had been treating the symptoms of the disease, but not the root cause. In an ironic twist, I could continue only addressing the specific problems—that is, the symptoms—of each restaurant I visited and make some great TV while I was at it. And since the restaurant had just been given the benefit of a massive plug on national television, they'd get a nice little bump to their bottom line. But that would only work in the short term. It would simply be a matter of time before they'd fall back on old habits because the bruised ego would rise up and demand validation. Unless I could dig deeper with each owner and get the real answer to the question of why they were acting this way, I wouldn't be able to help them long term.

This revelation completely changed my approach to the show and how we filmed it. Each episode from that day forward contained heart-to-heart conversations where we set aside the blame game and attempted to dig into the underlying issues.

I was worried about it at first. I'm not a psychiatrist and I can't diagnose anyone. But as I started heading down this route,

I realized that if I could spend the time to really connect with the restaurant owners and show them that I genuinely cared about their success and not just getting a good made-for-TV moment out of the exchange, then they would open up and see me for what I am: a knowledgeable veteran of their industry and a kindred spirit who understands what really drives people.

None of these folks—not even the meanest and nastiest of the bunch—were bad people. They were hurt. They were scared. They had so fully invested themselves in their work they were terrified that if an idea didn't work out, it didn't mean it was a bad idea and time to try something new—it meant that *they* were bad. And if their ideas didn't matter, then they didn't matter.

Long story short, the approach worked. Once I could see their stubbornness through this new lens, it was my gateway to being able to not just help them through the short-term crisis but also lead them to long-term success.

Appropriately, the restaurants weren't the only ones ideally positioned for the long haul, but the show itself owes its longevity to this approach. I was right in supposing that there were only so many times people would tune in to see the fireworks of a screaming match and a renovation. Sensationalism can get you some attention in television, but it can't get you the kind of loyalty we've enjoyed in primetime. Our viewers wanted something real, something they could identify with that resonated in their own lives.

Which brings me to some questions for you: What changes has your ego prevented you from making? Think hard about the mistakes you seem to make over and over again. Not just in your work but in your personal life. Are you someone who never seems to be able to stick to a diet and exercise regimen?

Constantly gets into the same fight with your spouse? Can't get good work out of your employees?

It's not a catchall, but you'd be surprised how much can be solved with an honest examination of your ego and how much attention and validation it demands.

While you're engaged in this moment of self-reflection, look back at your own career path. Are you someone who enjoyed a lot of success early? Or have you had to scratch and claw for every scrap from the table? It's not unusual for big egos to go hand in hand with the former; think of the trust-fund baby born on third who thought he hit a triple. But I encounter just as many big egos among the scrappy entrepreneurs, though it's borne from a different place; *I battled uphill my whole life and I got this far, so who are you to tell me I'm wrong?*

Dismantling either version of ego takes a willingness to be honest with yourself. In my mind, the great equalizer is acknowledging the fact that luck plays a role in all our journeys. The trust-fund kids usually need a swift kick in the ass and a reminder that they wouldn't have a fraction of the great opportunities afforded to them without their parents' money. Taking any position at a company not owned by a family member will usually provide this kick in the ass.

The fighters, meanwhile, need to remember that the success they've enjoyed isn't due entirely to their own hard work. For one thing, while I work incredibly hard, I've met people who work a lot harder than I do, yet they haven't enjoyed as much success as I have. Why? Because hard work and success do not share a one-to-one input-to-output relationship. Luck—specifically, where you were born, your innate abilities, social skills, charisma, access to education and opportunity—has a lot to say about how far you will be able to advance your career.

I'm a firm believer that most obstacles can be overcome with a strong enough work ethic, but I can't imagine enjoying the same level of success if I had been born in a developing country. There is simply no amount of hard work that would have ever given me the access to the kinds of opportunities I needed.

So if trust-fund kids have nothing to be proud of for having massive opportunities handed to them and hard work can't do it alone, then neither group has any business developing egos about where they are.

The Instagram hustle-meisters, of course, tell a different story.

Luck's got nothing to do with it, they say.

Just work, work, work, work, work, and then, one day . . . boom. You've made it.

Fascinating, isn't it? The notion that luck plays a role in virtually every other facet of life but . . . *not* in success? I'm not being coy or just trying to play devil's advocate. I understand what's at the core of a mantra like this; it's a call to work harder. But a lot of young entrepreneurs take it to heart—to the point where they feel a need to diminish or villainize other successful people who they deem "just got lucky."

Are you that insecure? That egotistical that your success is somehow tarnished if you admit that chance played a role?

Instead, I say do this: Don't push luck away. Embrace it. Tell yourself that you're lucky and expect the lucky breaks. Luck isn't some totally random phenomenon or the opposite of hard work; it's hard work's twin sibling. It's what shows up when you don't stop working.

Luck is all around you. Don't begrudge luck and feel a need to say, "No, actually, I did this all on my own." If you're reading this, you're lucky to be literate, lucky to have the gift of sight . . . lucky to be breathing at all. Luck is an incredible blessing. I look at my wife and my daughters and I'm reminded every day that my greatest accomplishment was getting lucky enough to have them in my life. So drop the pretense and ditch the ego. Embrace your luck for as long as it lasts. Remember: We're all just a heartbeat away from eternity.

EGO
RESTAURANT: IMPOSSIBLE CASE STUDY

Momma Pearl's Cajun Kitchen

This was one of the strangest experiences I've had on *Restaurant: Impossible*. Momma Pearl's Cajun Kitchen in Colorado Springs was $158,000 in debt and losing $4,000 a month. Yet the kitchen was clean and, by all outward appearances, professional. I watched a service and customers didn't have to wait. Right off the bat, three of the worst problems I typically encounter on the show—filthy, slow, chaotic—were ruled out.

So where was the problem? Look no further than head chef and owner Robert Brunet, who made me so angry during our initial meeting that I told him I simply didn't like him. This was supposed to be Cajun food—an homage to Robert's upbringing in Louisiana—but it was flavorless and unremarkable. The restaurant itself looked like a typical sports bar. Turns out it had been one previously. Now a supposedly Cajun restaurant lived in this setting, making for a bizarre disconnect. Worse still, the menu, signage, and even the catering van were plastered with a cartoon caricature of "Chef BB," the name Robert preferred to go by.

Through tears, Robert's wife and co-owner Becky explained that Chef BB was Robert's alter ego, and it was this alter ego who really ran things. Chef BB couldn't be spoken to. His food was good, he said. His concept was sound. And he completely shut out input from his experienced staff and his wife. He then broke down in tears when I told him he was failing. No, he insisted, he was merely struggling. He just needed a little bit of help.

Robert wasn't hearing me and he wasn't hearing his wife, so I let him hear it from everyone else—his staff and family—who wrote down on index cards everything they liked about Robert, and everything they disliked about Chef BB. The positives boiled down to Robert being a good grandfather. The negatives were far more numerous and included words like *arrogant*, *fake*, *angry*, *distant*, *verbally abusive*, and, above all, *egotistical*.

In a breakthrough, Robert explained that he'd had a chip on his shoulder his entire life. The tenth of thirteen children, he was, for want of better words, the runt of the litter, picked last or not at all in sports. When he was in first grade, he was deemed—in the vernacular of the time—"retarded" and sent to special ed classes. But he wasn't developmentally disabled in any way. He went on to a successful career in software engineering, and, crucially, was able to do so because he ignored everyone who said he wasn't good enough, smart enough, or talented enough to make something of his life.

Here was a man whose ego had taken his entire life and business hostage. He was living inside a manufactured suit of armor that shut out all criticism. It had served him well to a point, but now that armor was no longer necessary and it threatened to destroy his life. Faced with the feedback from the people around him, he vowed to change, which only upset Becky even more, who pointed out that she'd been telling him about these problems for years. "This has to change," she said. "I can't be told to shut the fuck up anymore."

Day 2 went well, and Robert was armed with a new menu and a restaurant that actually reflected the type of cuisine he was serving. His future looked bright. He appeared to be a totally changed man, enthusiastic in the kitchen, generous with his staff, and receptive to suggestions and feedback from the talented people who worked there. Sales went up and Momma Pearl's enjoyed a second honeymoon period where it was the buzzy spot in Colorado Springs. The ego had been slain.

Or so it seemed. In probably the most depressing end-of-show title cards we've ever run, we were forced to tell viewers that after a few weeks, Chef BB had made a return. Sales slumped as a result and several employees had left. Becky, meanwhile, clung to the hope that Robert could still make a lasting change.

I've said it before but it bears repeating: I can lead a horse to water but I can't make it drink. The changes I introduce on the show can only save the business if the owners are committed to making them last. Successful business leaders cannot ride a roller coaster of emotions, swinging between extreme lows and highs and allowing their turbulent inner lives to infect the business. Egotism is a toxic force that can ruin any business, no matter how many things might otherwise be working in its favor.

Robert, or Chef BB really, was in an extreme low point when I found him and it had clear carryover to every important relationship in his life. He hadn't defeated the naysayers; the very existence of the alter ego was the clearest evidence that those naysayers still ruled his life. Every time he lashed out at his wife and staff was a sad reminder that he still had a lot of demons to exorcise. When he suddenly soared on Day 2 and seemed to embrace optimism and accountability, those demons were still waiting for him at the first sign of trouble, at which point his ego proved it wasn't dead but merely playing possum. When he hit bottom again, it's no wonder it spooked the staffers who felt they now had to leave.

There's a good man in there, but he still has plenty of work to do if he's going to save his business and his marriage. If he can remember that setbacks don't impugn his talent and work ethic—and that moments of triumph don't mean he's beyond criticism—he'll have a chance. Lord knows I'm rooting like hell for him.

BUSINESS CLICHÉS TO PUT TO PASTURE

Don't hide behind phony euphemisms

I've just suggested you embrace the notion that luck plays a significant role in your journey and that you shouldn't push it away. What you must push away are some very tired business clichés that can negatively affect the way you think. These terms are pervasive and pernicious, and distort our notions of what's achievable. Without further ado, here are the terms I'd love to see on the chopping block.

"Think outside the box."

Like a lot of tired maxims, this one is well intentioned. It's rooted in a basic, hard-to-argue-with idea that one should be original and try to do something new. But for entrepreneurs who are just starting out, this is one of the last things they need to hear. Why? Because you can't think outside the box until you've mastered what's inside the box. You wouldn't learn to play three chords on a guitar and then decide you've done all you can with guitars and need to invent a brand-new instrument. Similarly, I cringe whenever I hear someone use this phrase—which borders on the demonization of mastery—especially if it's from someone who has never owned a business before or spent a lot of time in a company at the executive (or, barring that, decision-making) level.

DO THIS INSTEAD: Don't cast aside tried-and-true methods of business planning because you—and the Instagram hustle gurus—have decided the old ways are no longer sexy. Sexy is nice, but it doesn't last forever. In the business world, a firm knowledge base accumulated over many years in the field is the only thing that's built to last. It's valid to look for new ways of doing things, but in order to be successfully unconventional, you ought to know the conventional so well that you could give a three-hour lecture on it.

"Go big or go home."

It's exciting to come out and make a big splash immediately. But if you've gone all in right off the bat, every early mistake can feel company-defining or world-ending.

DO THIS INSTEAD: Set yourself up for steady, sustained growth. In my experience, steadily building over time is the preferred route for many reasons, chief among them being the fact that you absolutely will make mistakes. If you've started small, those mistakes are manageable; you learn your lessons, make adjustments, and move on. This is why so many stores and restaurants have soft openings before their grand openings. No big announcements. Just a whispered word-of-mouth promotion to see how all the machinery works before the real stress test begins.

I've built all my businesses slowly. There are plenty of other celebrity chefs who were able to get more product into the marketplace a hell of a lot faster than I was. A lot of my friends would ask me why so-and-so is already on big-city billboards and already in every supermarket in the country while my stuff was only available in specific regions and had a very small marketing budget behind it. The answer is pretty simple: most other folks in my line of work sign licensing deals. They don't own the companies that develop, create, ship, and market the product. That's not a knock on them; it's what they've chosen to do. When it comes to certain products—such as the kitchen knives that bear my name—I've signed a few licensing deals. But I'm just as passionate about business as I am about food, and I've found it immensely satisfying to build my companies from the ground up. The ability to control the quality of every batch of

Irvine's Vodka and American Dry Gin from my distillery, develop new flavors of protein bars every year, and send new frozen foods to market only when I'm satisfied with the quality and not when the board of directors at some other company decides it's time, is incredibly important to me. If you desire the same level of control—not for the sake of the power itself but for its positive impact on the end product and the customer experience—then you're never going to be happy handing the reins over to other people and just slapping your name on the products when they're done. To be hands-on is to commit to slow and steady growth. Get comfortable with that fact, because there's no way around it.

"No risk, no reward."

On its face, I totally get this one. All businesses carry inherent risk, but this saying is thrown around so flippantly and is too often used as an excuse to forge ahead with a business plan that's riddled with holes. Once you start emptying savings accounts and maxing out lines of credit, this isn't theoretical anymore. This is your family's livelihood.

DO THIS INSTEAD: You should be doing everything in your power to mitigate risk, from hiring experienced people to buying enough insurance to cover potential disasters to having enough cash on hand to pay for the adjustments you'll undoubtedly need to make. The traditional way of thinking of risk mitigation is to diversify much in the same way you'd diversify your own personal investment portfolio. When it comes to your first business, however, diversification is antithetical to what should be your one relentless focus: specialization to the point where you can flawlessly execute one or a small handful of things and thus become known for that thing. Within your first business, risk mitigation should center around this theme: mitigate the risk of putting out a bad product and of your customers having a bad experience. Word of mouth has always been crucial to success, but as we've established, in the age of social media it's absolutely critical that your customers are consistently thrilled with their experience. Do your job well and your happy customers will turn into a massive unpaid marketing force, spreading the good news about you far and wide. Do it poorly and lousy Google and Yelp reviews aren't far behind. If you and your employees come to view each customer interaction as not just an opportunity to make money but a potential public relations liability, then you'll be much further along than most businesses in terms of managing risk.

Too many business owners begin to feel entitled to the customer's business. They get comfortable, stop innovating, and stop thinking about the experience from the customer's point of view. Even for beloved community cornerstones, this attitude is death, albeit a slow one. In a new business, this attitude is a quick death. Loyalty can't dwindle if it's never established.

"My door is always open."

I'm guilty of using this one myself. Wanting to be certain that no one on my team ever has a fear of contacting me with any issue, everyone on my team has my cell number, email address, home address, Zoom username, Twitter handle, and so on.

While they should feel comfortable reaching out, saying "my door is always open" just isn't true. My door is most definitely not open to talk through problem-solving or anything else when I'm filming a show or on a plane. That's kind of a problem, because most of the time I'm doing one of those two things. But, as established earlier, I've hired great people. Over time they've been able to read between the lines and realize that every effort should be made to solve a problem before it gets to my level. Not because I'm the king and don't want to be bothered—I want nothing more than to jump in and help with everything—but there's only one of me and I can't get into the minutiae of one problem when I'm knee-deep in something else that demands my full attention.

Do I regret telling my folks that the door is always open? Well, I'll put it this way: "Only contact me if you absolutely have to" sounds terrible, even if it happens to be true most of the time. So I'd rather err on the side of acting more available than is realistic than make them think that I'm a sleeping dragon who can't be woken.

Over time I've remedied this and have pretty much retired the phrase (though I still say it sometimes out of pure muscle memory).

DO THIS INSTEAD: These days, I've turned the concept around and I go to them. The open-door policy in reverse has worked wonders. My employees get calls at random times—usually when I'm waiting in an airport—and I give them an opportunity to sound off about anything that's on their minds. You need to be reasonable and respect boundaries, of course. I always ask whether now is a good time or if they're with their families or having dinner, and I make it clear that it's fine if they're doing something else. The point is: Don't leave it up to your employees to decide when to break the boss's concentration with a question—or ruin their day with bad news.

"Let's pivot to . . ."

In recent years I've heard the term "pivot to video" enough times that I'm immediately suspicious of anyone who says the phrase. The word "pivot" is doing an awful lot of heavy lifting here. When you say, "We need to pivot to . . ." and then name something that's not already within your company's expertise—and by definition it probably isn't, otherwise you'd already be doing it—then what you're really saying is, "We need to develop entirely new skill sets and workflows and probably hire a bunch of new people to get this totally unrelated project off the ground."

Think about it: "Pivot to video" means hiring camera operators, editors, and producers. Doesn't sound like a pivot to me, but a radical transformation of your company's mission. If you don't currently employ any of those people, then you mean to retask and train people who are currently doing other things. That's a massive undertaking!

It's an insidious cliché because it allows the boss to hide how much work needs to be done behind a seemingly innocuous phrase. It takes the onus off you—the person who would rightly be tasked with developing the plan that will allow the company to "pivot"—and puts it on your employees. Struggling companies "pivot" all the time, chasing one trend after another.

DO THIS INSTEAD: If you need to "pivot," that's fine. But be honest about what that really means and have realistic expectations for how quickly it could be implemented.

BECOME A STUDENT FOR LIFE

Why constant learning is required for sustained success

I don't care what you can do once or sometimes, and your customers don't, either. A lot of young entrepreneurs—especially in the restaurant business—confuse having done something exceptional with *being* exceptional, a nasty trap that only leads to disappointment. Anyone can make a great dinner. Give me a few hours standing over the shoulder of an average guy whose culinary knowledge begins at flipping burgers and ends at making pancakes from a box mix, and nine times out of ten I could coach him into cooking something worthy of rave reviews from the judges on *Chopped*. But that wouldn't make him a chef, because, obviously, what you've done once under a watchful eye doesn't mean a damn thing. Let's take it further: you wouldn't hire an accountant who is great with numbers *on occasion* or go to a doctor who *usually* performs successful surgery. Hell, you don't even want to get lunch at a place with spotty execution.

When my stomach is rumbling, I'm not necessarily looking for food that's great or even particularly interesting; I'm looking to get *fed*. Most people feel the same way; if your mom-and-pop shop can't be consistent, there's nothing wrong with hitting the McDonald's drive-thru. It may never be great, but dammit, at least people know what they're getting.

These examples underscore a point that not enough people take to heart: Success is not a destination where one arrives. It is an ongoing journey of learning, practicing, and refining. When you finally approach what could be considered mastery, that's not a time to rest on your laurels. It's actually a dangerous time when arrogance can supplant fundamentals. Arriving at this moment is the very moment it's time to refamiliarize yourself with the basics. Regardless of the profession you're in, no one is ever so good at something that they can't benefit from continuing education, including refresher courses.

Teaching others is a great way to stay in touch with the fundamentals. When I train new restaurant staff, it requires me to explain every recipe from the ground up and verbalize why we do things a certain way, and it winds up helping me because the process keeps those fundamentals top of mind. While no one is totally immune from regression, the stronger your base of knowledge, the less likely it is that your skills will diminish.

Whatever your field, commit to being an expert in it and staying on the bleeding edge of the latest research and techniques. Don't be happy with having done something really well in the past and think that entitles you to future success. The ideal businessperson is one with a strong base in classic, established knowledge and a firm handle on what's new. The former actually helps inform the latter; the more you know about what has worked in the past, the better you'll be at deciphering which of the latest trends is bound to be a flash in the pan that won't hold up in the long run.

The most successful people I know never viewed their education as a thing that ended upon graduation. They are all students for life, voraciously studious in their fields, yet, even with years of success under their belts, humble enough to learn new things and accept that even though they've been getting along just fine, there might be a better way.

It sounds simple but having great talent and a commitment to learning is an uncommon combination of traits because ego grows with success and tends to get in the way of staying humble. I don't laud humility merely as an altruistic value, but as a good business practice. If your lack of humility stops you from learning and improving, it's not just an unpleasant character trait—it's a liability. This dynamic rears its ugly head constantly on *Restaurant: Impossible*. Sure, the owner wanted help, but for some reason they always imagine that their signature dish will be the one that will escape criticism. (Some do! Just not very often.)

Another reason people hesitate to continue their education is because the word "education" itself is loaded with a formal connotation—sitting at a desk, taking notes, passing exams, earning an official certificate that proves you know what you're talking about. Education needn't be formal. In fact, if you're running your own business or working full time, continuing to pursue a formal education, while not impossible, is incredibly difficult. Staying on top of the latest research and trends in your field or taking one class at a time is a much more manageable endeavor.

Moreover, I'm pretty liberal with what I consider education. Attending conferences, networking, and talking to other experts in your field—asking pointed questions and really taking note of their answers—are all forms of education. Hell, these days the simple act of picking up a book—even one unrelated to your field—while not technically education, is good for the mind, stimulating it in ways that our new national pastime—doom scrolling on our phones—never could. The former is meditative and relaxing and is proven to help you better empathize with others, while the latter is merely anxiety-inducing after a few minutes.

One of the most effective ways I've committed to being a student for life is to constantly meet new people. When you travel as much as I do, one of the things that compounds the excitement of waking up in a new place is the promise that the new day will bring new people into your life—and every person you meet could teach you in some unexpected way, possibly by doing something exceptional that you wish to emulate, possibly by their errors and lack of grace. The point is: when you reframe everyday interactions and happenstance as possible teachers, you transform your world into a classroom.

I assembled my team in just such a way. Every time I met someone who I felt was very talented, I spoke with them at length and tried to figure out what made them so good at what they do. My very best "teachers" got hired—not just so I could harness their talent and turn it into productivity that would help the company, but also so they could continue to teach me. To a person, I'm sure all of my employees would tell you that I've taught them a lot. Not all of them might know how much they've taught me—but I do.

Becoming a student for life is another way of declaring that you'll never settle. Of acknowledging your limitations and flaws and committing to eliminating or minimizing them. Not only is this for the benefit of self-improvement, but it's for the health of your bottom line. Recognizing that you have more to learn gives you a leg up on your competition. Always.

EIGHT

Win the Day

Setting daily goals that add up to big wins

I like to think of my work not only in terms of how much I'm getting done over the course of a week, a month, or a year, but in terms of how much I'm getting done every single day. Yes, it's imperative to have the long view of things and to keep your eyes on the big picture—and yes, shit happens and you're going to have days that don't go your way—but I think you need to be able to do both things at the same time: keep both the macro and micro in focus.

I've met too many people who will lose the first few hours of their day to assorted unforeseen variables and all too readily accept it, lose the whole damn day, and lean on the notion that whatever work they don't get done today they'll just make up at a later date. Of course any work you don't get done today can be done tomorrow, but the work that you're making up at that later date is taking the place of the stuff that you should have been doing on that later date. If you've got a big project on your hands like opening a restaurant, the snowball effect can be considerable.

Think of this way: in TV, typically if you lose a day of filming, the whole episode remains a day behind schedule until you're finished. The hours of footage that need to be captured can't simply be made up. That's a hardline example, but in other lines of work where you might be able to "stack" tasks for an intensified workload to make up the lost time, you're still not working in an optimized environment; you've sacrificed steady progress and invited errors into your work by jamming too much into too small a time frame.

I think most people should be familiar with the principle by now. When the coronavirus pandemic forced most of us to work from home amid the myriad distractions of screaming kids and noisy neighbors, almost none of us were working to our full potential on a daily basis. Sure, you finished the project that was due Friday, but you did most of it on Thursday night after juggling too many other responsibilities in the first part of the week when deadline pressure didn't force you to move quickly.

The crunch-time cycle is a dangerous habit to fall into—not just because it can produce flawed work but because it leads to burnout and, worst of all, a false sense of security that no matter how far you fall behind, you can always make it up at the last minute.

In short, the micro becomes the macro. The small habits are everything. And with that in mind, you need to look at how you can "win" each day.

Here's how I win each day:

1. The moment you wake up, take a deep breath and say thank you for the gift of another new day. Gratitude is the root of all prosperity, and since no day is

guaranteed to us, we need to express gratitude even for a lousy day, which beats the hell out of not having a day at all.

2. Once you've said thanks, set your priorities and intentions for the day. I'm not talking about etching out a to-do list. This is bigger than whatever errands you need to run or the emails you need to reply to. I'm talking about making a conscious effort to prioritize your big dreams and goals. What steps will you take today toward opening that business or turning around the one you've already got? Remember that the micro becomes the macro, so even a baby step toward a big goal is important. If it's a restaurant you dream of owning, write out your ideal dinner menu. If it's a brick-and-mortar retail store or online retailer, list out what kind of inventory you want to carry, and sketch out some logo or signage ideas.

3. Do something physical. You may not love to pump iron the way I do or even have a gym membership. That's fine. Go for a brisk walk or a bike ride. Do a short circuit of sit-ups, push-ups, and bodyweight squats. Whatever it is, get it done early if you can. The health benefits are important, but for our purposes here we can ignore the long-term ramifications and just know that blood flow is crucial to your workflow! Reading books and articles or listening to podcasts and lectures are great ways to stimulate the brain, but nothing can ever replace exercise. The brain isn't just the ideas that flow

through it; it's an organ like any other that needs the oxygen and nutrients that the blood provides. So, get that blood moving.

For me, most days begin with me getting all three of these things done in quick succession: I say my thanks, mentally make note of my priorities, and then hit the gym. Most of my best ideas will then come to me while I'm warming up. If the idea is burning hot, I'll make notes on my phone right then or call the principals involved in the project I'm brainstorming around.

After I hit the shower, I get dressed in my "uniform," which for years has been a blue T-shirt, blue jeans, and black loafers. If you just imagined that my closet looks like Batman's where it's just hanger after hanger of the same exact thing, you're not far off. You might further deduce that I'm not particularly passionate about fashion, and you'd be correct on that count, as well. But it's not that I'm apathetic about my appearance. There are two things at work here: 1) Studies have shown that our ability to make decisions diminishes as the day goes on. So why waste precious decision-making abilities early in the morning, hemming and hawing over what to wear? Just wear the same thing every day! Or at least lay out your clothes the night before. 2) Branding. Steve Jobs wore the same thing every day, and it wasn't just for the brainpower-preserving effects. Put simply: I'm more recognizable like this, kind of like a walking logo. It's good for my businesses and easier for me.

Again, you don't need to pull this particular move unless it really interests you, but it should make you think of ways of simplifying your life. Think hard: Which parts of your daily routine could be stripped down or streamlined so that they're not getting in the way of the work you need to do—and, more importantly, the fun you need to have? (After all, what's the point of all this hard work if you're not enjoying it?) This could mean prepping your meals the night before or "outsourcing" unpleasant household tasks. In my experience, most people think they can't afford to have someone clean their house/take out the trash/feed their turtles until they look into it. Then, through simple budgeting, they realize that by nixing a couple bottles of wine and canceling that streaming service they hardly have time to watch anymore, all of a sudden they can afford this newfound luxury. (Tim Ferriss's excellent *4-Hour Workweek* is a compendium of such ideas, helping people simplify their routines with everything from secretarial work to personal chefs.) Then, once they've offloaded some of those menial tasks, they're free to think big, chase their goals, and enjoy life.

Trust me, once you get a taste of living this way, you won't think of it as a luxury. You'll realize it's too costly to go back to the old way of doing everything yourself.

PROCRASTINATION

The true nature of the beast we all battle

Procrastination isn't what they've told you. It's not laziness. It's not a lack of motivation. It's not even a lack of inspiration. Procrastination is fear. Nothing more, nothing less.

Lack of action toward a goal or a new idea is a self-defense mechanism against the fear that your new idea is no good or that you're not the right person to execute it and your finished product will suck.

When we first get an idea, it's perfect. All the possibilities are before us: we can see people lined up around the block for it, happy customers praising its life-changing impact, news stories about how it swept the nation or the world, checks with a bunch of zeros on the end. It's a lovely moment when our brains are awash in dopamine and it seems like nothing can go wrong. Call this phase infatuation. It might pass, right?

Well, a few days have gone by and you still can't stop thinking about your idea. You start thinking this idea might really be "the one" and it's time to get a move on and make a commitment to this thing.

Boom. You take the plunge. You dive into researching your idea and start mapping out your plans for global domination. It's just you and a pad of paper right now. Such humble beginnings! Won't this be such a neat little moment to tell everyone about when you're a guest on *The Tonight Show*?

Then a few weeks go by. You're into the nitty-gritty. Honeymoon's over now. All that's left: the seriously hard work of bringing this idea from a daydream into solid reality. The initial infatuation is a distant memory. Oh man, what you wouldn't give for a hit of that dopamine right now to propel you through this new drudgery.

Problem is, the more work you do, the more problems come to the fore. You soon realize your original business plan isn't feasible. The materials you wanted to use are too expensive. The market for your grand design is perhaps smaller than originally estimated. Then, a real kick in the teeth: You discover that someone else tried something just like this a few years ago and lost their shirt on the endeavor. The whole thing crashed and burned within a few months.

Maybe this idea wasn't "the one" after all. Maybe it's time you and this idea went your separate ways.

Hey. It happens every day. No big deal. Really.

What's important right now is the story you tell yourself about this experience. This little exercise didn't fall apart because you're not smart enough or skilled enough. It wasn't even a bad idea. Just maybe not the right idea for this particular moment and this particular place. You will live to fight another day. You may even live to revive this idea in the right moment.

We've all had an experience just like this, even if it wasn't a business or product idea. Could've been—as the above metaphor is constructed—a romantic entanglement. Since we're adaptive creatures with decent self-preservation instincts, we emerge from any difficult experience—physical or emotional—with new coping mechanisms.

And if you're like most people, you won't just be more thorough and careful with your next big idea. You will probably . . . procrastinate.

Doesn't that make perfect sense? When you think about it, procrastination is a great way to protect an idea that's still in its infancy. If you don't begin work on the idea, none of the aforementioned problems can reveal themselves to you. This is an absurd thought for the conscious mind to have, but you can be sure it's there in your subconscious. That's why it's perfectly normal to have ambitions the size of the moon, but when you sit down to actually work on them, your brain becomes a kaleidoscope of jumbled bullshit that has absolutely nothing to do with your hopes and dreams. You cleared your calendar to get to work but now you can't stop checking Facebook every fourteen seconds, and . . . *Oh crap, did I forget to clean the litter boxes? I think the car needs an oil change. Gee, I am kinda hungry . . . I better go make a sandwich before I get started*, and on and on.

Sound familiar? Maybe too familiar? You're far from alone. Everyone does this in some form or another. Again, your first step needs to be to resist the initial urge to beat the crap out of yourself. If you knock yourself down for the count, who's going to get you out of this mess?

Once you catch yourself in the midst of one of these cycles, it's time to take immediate action to break it. And the key word there is "action." I have a bias toward action. I'm much more inclined to start doing, not sit around and theorize for days on end. Having a plan is good. Obsessing over the plan and revising it a thousand times before you actually do a damn thing is less good. Your plan is never going to be perfect. No matter how much you refine the plan, it will have flaws, and action tends to be the only way to reveal most of those flaws.

You may not have been born with a bias toward action, but you can develop one. A good place to start is by reframing your personal concept of failure. For starters, stop making this so personal. If something doesn't work, it doesn't mean you're an idiot. It just means you haven't found the right way to do it yet. And lucky for you, your latest failure armed you with precious knowledge about how not to approach the project; you can now mount another attempt all the wiser and more experienced.

Every moment you spend scrolling Twitter and other meaningless nonsense, you're robbing yourself of those crucial experiences of failure, which are really just opportunities to learn and get smarter and better equipped to turn your grand visions into concrete reality.

A note on procrastination while we're on the topic: If you're going to do it, do it like you mean it! Go for a walk or a bike ride, pick up a book you've always meant to read, or sit your ass down and watch a whole damn movie. Do something that might actually inspire you to get going. Whatever you do, don't waste it staring at your phone. Exposing yourself to a bunch of other people's ridiculous opinions is a great way to piss yourself off and ensure you don't get anything done. And remember: Around here, we get shit done.

PERSISTENCE

It's just another word for faith

Another reason you don't want to sit there and beat the crap out of yourself: Life is gonna do plenty of that without your help. If you want to achieve something great, you have no choice but to persist.

Another title for this section could be "What you can learn from Walt Disney." I like to remind people of his humble roots because Walt Disney the cultural icon is so firmly enshrined in the heart of American popular culture that his struggles and failures—and superhuman persistence in the face of them—aren't just overlooked; most of the ardent fans of his artistic creations aren't even aware of them. Yet it's hard to enumerate how many times his studio and all his grand aspirations stood a hair's breadth away from being destroyed.

Walt possessed many of the qualities that I've championed in this book. He was a man of incredible passion and vision, and an inspiring leader and communicator who, for most of his career, enjoyed fervent loyalty and devotion from his staff.

But there was nothing preordained about his success. Walt came from a poor family, used art as a means of escape, and attempted to realize his dream of creating his own animation studio with the help of his brother Roy, who begged and scraped together loans and investments from myriad sources in tiny amounts, often defaulting on those obligations and being forced to start all over.

Even when Walt met with success and was a known and revered figure in Hollywood, riding on the heels of the smash hit *Snow White and the Seven Dwarfs* with close to a thousand workers in his employ, the fate of the company rode on virtually every feature release after that one. He set the bar so high for what he wanted to accomplish with each film that he would constantly tinker, reworking whole sequences of animation that had already been painstakingly finished. It was wildly expensive to make films the way Walt wanted to make them, but in his mind, there was no point in putting out a product that anyone else could deliver. Exceptionalism was the purpose of everything he did.

To Walt, money was simply a tool, a means to an end. He reinvested nearly all his profits back into the studio to further the animation medium and enhance the company's reputation. His perfectionism and ambition led his company to the brink of bankruptcy on many occasions. Yet for all his intractability as an artist, he was not totally oblivious to reality, and eventually found a way to leave the bar incredibly high for animated features, but lower it when the times absolutely demanded it to keep his employees working. During World War II, for instance, the market forces of the time essentially required him to repurpose the whole mission of the studio from one that produced whimsical animated shorts and features to one that almost exclusively produced training films and propaganda.

When the war ended, he came back to what motivated him in the beginning. By remaining laser-focused on his vision—taking it as an article of faith that producing a high-quality product would win out in the end—he always found a way to pull the company through hard times.

There's inspiration to take from the story, certainly. Unflagging persistence and devotion to your passion is an admirable quality and one to be emulated. But there are pitfalls to be aware of, as well.

Because if you look at the Disney story and your only takeaway is that you need to stay the course and keep pushing, you're only seeing what you want to see: a vague promise that there's a pot of gold at the end of the rainbow. Yes, the gold is there if you have a great idea and steadfast work ethic, but you also need to be prepared to endure real hardship. Today, the fact that Walt's earlier studios failed is an interesting footnote in his biography. But the realities that can accompany losing it all—namely, homelessness and hunger—are nothing to be trifled with.

I see this every time I visit a failing business on *Restaurant: Impossible*. People get into a business because they have excitement and passion, but when things start to go south, they meet with hardship that they were never prepared for and it exacerbates the situation. In addition to having to take out additional loans, lay off staff, and revamp a menu, there's a higher mental and emotional toll because unexpected pain is so much harder to cope with.

Maybe you can honestly say you're prepared to face such consequences if you come up short. Fair enough. But what about everyone in your orbit? Is your spouse prepared? How about your children? Your siblings? Your parents? Anyone else affected by your decisions needs to be taken into consideration.

This is doubly true if, like many entrepreneurs, you've looked to your family for early funding (though I've cautioned against it for a host of reasons). You owe it to yourself and everyone in your life to consider the worst-case scenario before starting up a new business. What is your backup plan if you wash out? Will you try to open another business or will you change career paths entirely?

Walt Disney was a great artist and visionary, but people remember his name because his real superpower was the ability to pivot from one defeat to his next attempt without missing a beat or losing his enthusiasm.

Hardship will come. It doesn't matter how talented you are or how good your plan is. There are always going to be variables that simply cannot be accounted for. Mentally prepare for that. Be honest with yourself and those around you. And remember that success isn't guaranteed. If that only excites you more and hardens your resolve, I'm happy to call myself your brother in spirit. I'm not a gambler, but I'd be lying if I didn't say that risk made all this so much more exciting—to say nothing of the fact that the specter of failure drives me to produce my best work.

On the topic of risk, though, it should be noted that not everyone in your life is going to be comfortable with it. That's why it is essential to surround yourself with the right people. We're social creatures, after all, and since we will invariably pick up the habits of the people we spend the most time with, it would behoove us that those people possess habits that will reinforce good work habits and productivity, ultimately furthering our goals.

This is such an obvious piece of advice when it comes to hiring and choosing partners, investors, and other collaborators. The downsides to bad hires and partnerships are steep. The upside to great hires and partnerships are equally steep in the other direction.

But I say that you need to take this concept a step further. Look closer to home. Look at your friends. And as difficult as it may be, look at your family.

Whoa, Robert. Just what the hell are you insinuating here? That I ditch my family if they don't support my business?! You monster!

OK, first of all, I'm not a monster, though I have been called worse. (You try telling a chef at a failing Italian restaurant that his grandmother's marinara has too much garlic. Never a fun conversation.)

Second, I'm not advocating that anyone abandon their family if they're not supportive enough. But take inventory of all personalities around you. You probably have a cousin, a sibling, a parent—possibly a spouse—who, against all odds, always seems to be able to find the clouds on a sunny day. People who focus on the risk and consequences over the potential rewards. Who emphasize difficulty over possibility. They just can't be grateful for the day that is in front of them. Something about that day, as sunny and breezy as it is, should be better.

These folks might be delightful otherwise. They could love you and support you in dozens of other ways. But their risk aversion and negativity—which has held them back in their own careers—is seriously contagious and, just as you would treat anyone with an airborne illness, you need to limit your exposure to them. Arnold Schwarzenegger famously gave no quarter in the gym. Not to people who were weaker than him (please, just about everyone was weaker than him), but to people who were negative. Either you added to the camaraderie and energetically supported everyone else in the training session or you were out.

It should be noted that this is a two-way street. You can't just expect to take. You need to give back to those around you in equal measure. For starters, it's the right thing. For another, why would everyone keep giving to you if they get nothing in return?

In the Schwarzenegger example, everybody won. Not only did he get the benefit of having a devoted support group, the weaker lifters were also elevated, inspired to chase his greatness and given the motivation to do more than they thought possible.

Now, what to do if the negativity in your life is coming from a spouse? That's a much trickier situation. It's easy enough to keep putting off that visit to your brother-in-law's house. But when you share a bed with the person who can't find anything good to say about your new project, then you may have bigger problems that would be better addressed by someone with different expertise. In the meantime, do everything you can to protect your ambition from scrutiny. Keep it to the people who do believe in you and support you. Let it blossom. Let it grow. Turn skeptics into believers. Nothing wins converts like the success of a great finished product.

PERSISTENCE

RESTAURANT: IMPOSSIBLE **CASE STUDY**

The Ship Inn

It's important to look at the flip side of every issue, so if ever there was a cautionary tale about the dangers of the persistence-above-all mindset, I found it at the Ship Inn in Exton, Pennsylvania. A historic tavern that dates back to 1795 and boasts George Washington, Andrew Jackson, and Jackie Onassis among its guests, the Ship Inn is now a steak and seafood restaurant run by Michael Person. An experienced hospitality manager, Michael ran the Ship Inn successfully for many years. He bought the building in the early 2000s and for a fifteen-year stretch pulled in as much as $2.1 million annually.

Over time, however, business slowed, then slumped, then nearly disappeared altogether. Frantic to stay afloat, Michael remortgaged his home to meet payroll and pay his taxes and utilities, but without making any changes to the restaurant's menu, décor, or operations, he continued to hemorrhage money. When I arrived, Michael was $895,000 in the hole. Moreover, he hadn't been honest with his wife, Gertie, about the situation and had taken out the mortgage on their home without her knowledge. Perhaps most embarrassingly, Gertie was a successful restaurant owner who ran her own place down the road—and she refused to visit the Ship Inn, saying it made her sad to be there.

I could empathize. It was obvious to me why the Ship Inn was sinking; everything was old, and not in a good way. Again, there is a very big difference between vintage and dated. Vintage is cozy. Dated is stuffy. The dining room was lined with old carpet and cluttered with booth seats that looked like roller coaster benches. White tablecloths helped further rob it of character, which the building actually had in spades. The servers looked like time travelers from the 1980s—black slacks and white button-downs— and the menu felt just as out of place, devoid of a single vegetarian option or anything a younger crowd would come out for; what I sampled would barely pass muster with the AARP early-bird crowd.

In this instance, Michael was at least partially victimized by his own long history of success. When you make good money for a fifteen-year run, it's hard to abandon the ideas that got you there. I'm sure that in Michael's mind, a reversal of fortune was always just around the corner. So he doubled down not just in his investment but also in the way he pressed his employees, who were so badly micromanaged they strove to survive their shifts without getting yelled at, never mind giving customers a positive experience.

It showed. We canvassed the town and interviewed people who had eaten at the Ship Inn; since the place had been around forever, almost everyone in town had tried it at some point. Indeed, most of the people we interviewed had eaten there multiple times—but none of them had done so recently because lousy experiences had chased them away.

Michael needed a serious wake-up call and I gave him that; we brought his dining room, his servers (including their uniforms), and his menu into the twenty-first century, empowering his executive chef to get creative and not chase trends but at least stay in touch with current tastes. A humbled Michael vowed to take advice from Gertie, and the bar was renamed in her honor.

This was a unique episode for a few reasons. A lot of failing restaurants never knew success or only flirted with it briefly. Michael's ownership of the Ship Inn had been mostly successful, never mind the steady two hundred years of operation before that. The building itself was also beautiful with a wonderful history. I shudder to think of all that might have gone to waste if Michael hadn't applied to be on the show. To his credit, he finally hit the panic button and called for help, though he almost did so too late.

I think Michael's story can be a lesson for anyone who thinks sticking to their guns and working harder is the only way out of a jam. Hard work doesn't help if you're not working smart, and there's no shame in asking for help. Michael was married to a successful restaurateur! Pride, and a stubborn belief in the power of persistence, nearly sank him. Don't let it sink you.

NEVER TOO HIGH, NEVER TOO LOW

*Why an even-keeled long-term approach
is the only one to take*

While passion is the beating heart that will sustain your idea through various ups and downs, you can't afford to put yourself in a position where your day-to-day excitement dictates your confidence and faith in the project as a whole.

I'll borrow a sports metaphor to make the point. Steph Curry is one of the greatest basketball players ever, but even he hits a bad stretch now and then where he's not shooting well. Maybe it's a quarter, a half, a full game, or even a couple of games. Not likely for him to be off for such a long time, but just go with me for a minute. If he's in a rut, he may look at the film and realize he needs to make an adjustment or two, but he won't begin to question the very fundamentals that got him to where he is or doubt the fact that he's one of the best in the game. That's an example of never being too low. On the flip side of that, I'm sure he knows how to ride a hot streak where he feels like he can't miss; if he makes ten in a row, sure, he'll keep shooting, but he won't start taking crazy risks or chucking the ball from half-court. That's an example of never getting too high.

That's because Steph Curry's been playing basketball his whole life, and while he wants to perform at his peak every night, he knows that, like it or not, there will be rough patches, and the big picture becomes what he's really concerned with, namely how many championship rings he'll have when he retires.

Curry's approach to basketball is a smart approach for everything. Your business won't survive if you freak out every time there's a bit of volatility in your marketplace. For another example, a marriage that's redefined each day based on whether you had a perfect romantic dinner or a bad argument is destined to end in divorce. Everything has peaks and valleys, and you need to be able to step back and realize that all of them are temporary. The important question is where things trend over time.

My restaurants in Las Vegas and the Pentagon had to close during the early period of the coronavirus pandemic. While my other businesses—liquor, frozen foods, and protein bars—all saw new peaks during this time for obvious reasons, I still had to make a decision about the restaurants. There would be no shame in permanently shuttering them, especially early on when we had no idea how long the pandemic and its attendant lockdown might last. But I decided to keep them. Why? The long-term numbers told me to. Both restaurants had done great business and showed steady growth. Whenever we would be able to reopen them, there was no reason I could think of that those trend lines wouldn't resume. If anything, the initial return to indoor dining would provide a new peak—thanks to an anxious public that was bound to fill restaurants in record numbers as soon as they were able to—which would help alleviate some of the losses incurred during lockdown.

The new peak wasn't bound to last, either, but it doesn't matter—and that's the whole point. Highs and lows never last. Progress never happens in a straight line. Extend this thinking to every area of your business and not just your bottom line. Employee performance has peaks and valleys, as does product popularity and customer behavior. Don't mourn or rejoice in either instance. Just concern yourself with the overall trend.

NINE

Work-Life Balance

Making peace with the essential
trade-offs of an entrepreneur's life

It would seem unnecessary or redundant to point out that success in business requires a tremendous amount of work. After all, the advice I've offered thus far collectively points in the direction of many long hours and late nights. But I think there's a misconception among younger entrepreneurs that the hard work is temporary and that you can eventually get to a spot where you begin to coast. Maybe that's true of some businesses, but I have yet to encounter such a thing. It's certainly not true of working in television, the restaurant industry, frozen foods, or online media. Every single endeavor at which I've tried my hand has demanded elbow grease—if not literally in the form of sweat and sore muscles, then figuratively in that they've required constant learning and strategizing.

I would be further remiss to omit mention of the thing that has been the single greatest contributing factor to my success—and that is the fact that I love to work. I have always been possessed by big ambitions, and so I am eternally grateful that I was also blessed with a work ethic to match. Ambition is indeed an unwelcome visitor in the mind of a lazy person who will then ceaselessly figure out a way around the hard work that those ambitions demand. I pity those folks, truly, because if they could step outside themselves for just a moment, they'd see that the intense mental gymnastics they've engaged to try to avoid work use up just as much energy as doing the damn work itself.

Some have called me a workaholic and meant it as a pejorative, as in, a bias toward action is a defense mechanism—and just like any other addiction, being a workaholic is a way to push away emotions or avoid having to ponder mortality and other heavy subjects. They might have a point; Lord knows the second we stop working on *Restaurant: Impossible* and we do the big reveal, the tears flow easily enough on my end. Is it a cathartic release from all the hard work? Empathy and joy for the people who have a second shot? Or did the breakneck filming and renovation schedule force me to bury things I was already feeling? Maybe a little bit of each. But what this criticism misses is the fact that being a workaholic—as opposed to some other addiction—can actually yield a positive result. You might get addicted to your work, but at the end you get to bring something good into the world that wasn't there before.

While I was blessed with a love of work, there's hope for those who can't seem to resist the siren call of their couch cushions: work ethic can be learned. There is immense joy in completing difficult tasks. That joy is usually paired with pride tied to the end result—never mind writing a book or building a house, just think of how you feel when you finish putting together a kid's toy—or cathartic release: think of scrubbing your bathroom

WORK-LIFE BALANCE | 191

spotless. In either case, there's an endorphin rush, an evolutionary reward for doing the difficult, a chemical signal from Mother Nature to continue pushing us forward.

The trick, then, is to use your own willpower to provide the initial excitement to begin the difficult project. You need to remind yourself—and this is something I do every single day—that you're going to feel incredible when the work is done. It's a high that none of life's more easily attained, simple, guilty pleasures— food, booze, doom scrolling, pick your poison—could ever match because it's pure, and it's good for you! The high you get from a job well done is fully earned, wholly yours, and comes with none of the unavoidable trade-offs of eating crap, drinking alcohol, or procrastinating. And best of all: Hard work makes all those little rewards you want to give yourself exponentially more enjoyable and worth the wait.

Try this: When you wake up in the morning, as soon as you're done brushing your teeth, have a little chat with the person you see in the mirror. Get real close, look right into those eyes, and adjust the following monologue as you see fit: "You are going to go out there and kick ass in the way that only you and no one else on Earth can. It's going to be a lot of hard work, but it's going to feel so damn good to do it. Best of all: there is nothing you can't do."

You can get as lofty or as basic as you want. The point is that you psych yourself up and go get it done, whatever it may be. I'm not going to lie: mirror work is awkward as hell the first few times you do it, but like anything else that becomes a habit, the challenge fades. And you absolutely should do it, because it works! You believe what you say about yourself, so say really great, encouraging things, and aim as high as you want to. Why wouldn't you? We've just established there's nothing you can't do!

Being ready to work and actually doing the work, of course, are two different things. The best advice I can give here is to remember that this is all a marathon. Sprints (long days) will be needed along the way as you approach certain deadlines, but in terms of overall effort, choosing a sustainable pace can mean the difference between success and failure.

TRADE-OFFS

Saying yes to anything means saying no to something else

The notion of "having it all" was never meant to be insidious, yet I can't help but feel that's exactly what it's become. Americans are taught—through all forms of media—from a very young age that they have a right to it "all" and that getting it all is the clearest signal you can send to others that you are successful. Vital. That your life has meaning and importance.

Having it all has extended beyond the traditional hallmarks of keeping up with the Joneses. To wit, having the big house, fancy car, and fine clothes are now only one part of a psychological epidemic in which our eyes are bigger than our proverbial stomachs. Measures of success in American life have evolved. You can't just project that you're well-off or wealthy. You've got to simultaneously project that you're smart, popular, interesting, creative, and unique. Wouldn't hurt to have a ton of social media followers. A good-looking spouse and a few kids, too. Oh, and you should own the hot start-up and also have "work-life balance."

It's good to want things and to strive for a better life. But I don't think this kind of endless, spiraling desire that we are collectively experiencing leads anywhere good. I just see it leading to stress and anxiety and to an atomized attention span where everyone starts a dozen projects simultaneously and never finishes any of them. It leads to physical exhaustion and mental fatigue.

Because while we're climbing this gigantic, unwieldy mountain and collecting all this shit, we're also supposed to want work-life balance, which, when you're starting a business of your own, becomes a joke. Your business becomes your life. I should know. When I was first getting my culinary career off the ground, I was also getting my first marriage under way. It didn't last because it couldn't last. I was barely ever home. I was pulling eighteen-hour days in the kitchen and pitching TV shows and traveling the country.

The career I wanted was incompatible with some of the life choices I had made. My story has a happy ending, of course. I'm fortunate that I'm close to both of my daughters from my first marriage and I'm lucky as hell that I found my soulmate in Gail. But you have to understand that my love for Gail wouldn't have been enough if she didn't fully understand exactly what I wanted out of my career and know everything that that life entails. It works because Gail lives the same kind of life. A showbiz veteran, she knows all about living out of a suitcase, of spending so much time on airplanes that you wake up from a nap mid-flight and honestly forget where that plane is headed.

In sharing this, I'm hoping I can give you permission to say no to certain things in life. Things that might seem attractive, fun, or enjoyable, but ultimately aren't compatible with the big goals you've set for yourself.

Saying yes to your dream means saying no to a lot of the other little things that you'd also like to have. Having realized so many of my dreams, I can assure you that the sacrifices are worth it. Saying no used to be hard for me. It feels great now. I swear to you: you don't need even half the shit you think you're supposed to have. Less is most definitely more.

And the crazy part is this: in chasing the biggest dream and eschewing all else, you're going to wind up with so many of those other things by accident! A person who successfully chased down their dream and caught it is going to be interesting, creative, unique. You won't need to try to project any of that to try to get Instagram followers or to try to get someone to date you. It will just be part of who you are.

Chase the big thing. Say no to distractions. Work your ass off. You'd be shocked by how much of that ancillary stuff just happens to show up.

WORK-LIFE BALANCE
RESTAURANT: IMPOSSIBLE CASE STUDY

Grille No. 13

Besides saying no to external things you don't need in your personal life, a business leader sometimes needs to learn to say no to managing aspects of the business that no longer require their presence.

Enter Grille No. 13 in Waldorf, Maryland. When I visited there and met owner Katie Pierce, she provided me with a textbook definition of being spread too thin. She was a successful baker who pivoted to running an Irish American pub, but as her business mission expanded, she delegated nothing. She still baked cakes regularly—which she sold from the front of the house—and stepped into the line in the kitchen, ostensibly to help move things along faster.

In the world of software coding there's a term, "cruft," which perfectly encapsulates Katie's problem. "Cruft" is the word engineers use to refer to old code in the underlying program that no longer serves its original purpose. For instance, by the time you're using version 7.0 of a particular program, there's probably a lot of leftover code from previous versions lying underneath that has no function in the new version and that subsequent engineers simply built on top of. For a while you can get away with this; the new code simply supersedes the old. But as you continue to update the software, it's only a matter of time before this cruft gets in the way and slows things down.

What Katie needed to do was get into the code and dig out the cruft. In her case, she wasn't redesigning a piece of software from the ground up, but rebuilding her life. As she expanded from baker to restaurant owner and manager, to mother, everything suffered. She was still running around buying supplies, trying to handle all hiring and training for restaurant staff, still baking—and barely making any money at it—while her newborn daughter was at home with her husband because she spent twelve hours a day working at the restaurant.

To illustrate the point in terms I hoped she'd understand, I plopped a double layer cake in front of her and asked her to ice and decorate it for me in ten minutes. For a pro like her it wouldn't be a problem. Then I added another cake to the queue. Then I told her the toilet was backed up. Then I added another cake. Then I told her a customer was complaining because of hair in their food.

Needless to say, she couldn't handle the workload. She barely got one cake done, haphazardly at that, and the whole project failed as it was meant to. Then I told her that the undecorated cakes represented her pub, her bakery, and her family.

A teacher in her first career with experience creating lesson plans, she was armed with the skills to straighten this out and remove the old cruft from her life. She empowered and promoted a competent restaurant manager, hired a dedicated cake baker to come in two days a week, and in an immensely satisfying end credits title card, we informed viewers that she was home by seven o'clock every night to be with her family.

Think of Katie's situation as your business grows and expands. What is the cruft in your life? What needs to be deleted so that the new program can flourish? When you're used to being a one-person band, I know how hard it can be to let go, but remember that anything that someone else can be doing gives you more time to focus on the big picture. Delegating to people you trust will give your business a bright future to look forward to. It can also ensure you still have a family to come home to when the day is done.

IT'S NOT WHO YOU ARE, IT'S WHO YOU KNOW

Why it's true, and how to make it work for you

While you're out there chasing that big thing, you need to watch out for one more cliché, and this one is an old pessimist's standby, a built-in excuse for all manner of failures. It's so strongly worded, so damn sure of itself, so perfect in its structure, it practically makes you feel like a fool for even considering an attempt at breaking into a competitive field.

"It's not who you are, it's who you KNOW!"

OK. Let's run with that for a minute. Let's assume the premise of the argument is true, that there are certain fields that are so competitive you don't stand a chance without at least one strong personal connection. If you encountered such a reality, what would you do? Repeat the cliché to yourself and everyone at the dive bar as you wax poetic about why you never made anything of yourself? Or, gee, I dunno . . . would you maybe start trying to get to know some damn people in that field?

But shouldn't they want me for the value I can bring? Not the friends I have at the company?

I get it. You want to be recognized for your talent and work ethic. Networking or making friends to help you move up the ladder feels icky, maybe even like you're using them or perpetuating a rotten system. I won't lie: cronyism and nepotism are ugly aspects of the business world, and if either of these things ever stood in your way, it can feel like a betrayal of your own ethics to try to twist them in your favor. So let me be clear: that's the wrong way of thinking about this.

Instead, think of it this way: a company posts a job opening for a just-above-entry-level position and gets 250 cover letters and résumés within a few days. Now, they need the position filled as soon as possible. Do you think it's even feasible that this many applications would get a thorough review? Do you think the company bears some responsibility to the very notion of fairness that they scour all those résumés looking for the most talented, qualified applicant?

Or can you start to understand that looking through all those applications is a monumentally time-consuming task and that it would be wise to utilize some more realistic, common-sense criteria in the decision-making process? Say it's you conducting the search. You look at those 250 résumés, consider the decent-but-not-spectacular salary you'd be offering, and immediately toss the ones you deem overqualified—the folks with master's degrees and other people with so much experience you can't possibly imagine they'd be happy doing that particular job.

Boom. The pile is now cut in half.

As you go through the rest of the pile, you try to imagine not just who could do the job but who could be really happy in the role, who could grow into it, thrive, and maybe even take it beyond what you had originally intended. Hard to tell from résumés and cover letters, but you look for patterns. Then you finally happen upon one candidate who worked with an old colleague or classmate of yours. Now you call that old friend up and you get to have an honest conversation about what the applicant is really like, something that calling an officially listed reference doesn't really allow for.

The lowdown you get from that person isn't just positive—it's glowing. It's everything you wanted to hear: the candidate works their ass off, wants to learn, and, most crucially, is a true team player, pitches in well outside of their official job description, and contributes to a generally positive work environment.

Well, I don't know about you, but it sounds like this is the right person for the job. Sure, you'll interview a few more, but if you're being honest, it's just to have something to contrast against the candidate you already know you want.

Is it fair to the people who are getting called in for that purpose? Nope. Does it happen all the time? Sure does. But again—and I cannot stress this point enough—think about it from the employer's side. They see your résumé but they don't have a personal, trusted connection to any of your references. That means anything your references say about how you're such a hard worker and how much you love babies and baby seals and once donated one of your kidneys to a sick kitten in an incredibly risky cross-species transplant operation . . . it'll all be taken with a grain of salt. They *know* they can trust this other evaluation because they *know* the person who gave it.

Hence, the person who gets the job will be a beneficiary of that old cliché: it's not who you are, it's who you know.

Maddening to the other candidates, perhaps. But in the above example, with such an overwhelming number of applicants—as often happens, even for a job that isn't that great—isn't the hiring manager being a total buffoon if they *don't* hire the candidate on whom they have such great inside information?

Success of any kind, but especially success in business, is highly dependent on your ability to stop viewing occurrences such as the above example in terms of good and bad, right and wrong, fair or unfair. It simply is. That's the nature of your playing field, so get with it. Don't bemoan that reality sucks. Rid yourself of the notion that you have any right to fairness in any arena. The unfairness of this world begins at birth with whatever genetic lotto numbers you drew. Some people get to be big and strong. Others might be blessed with sensational beauty or a pitch-perfect singing voice. Still others have the brains to write epic, timeless novels or build rocket ships or cure diseases. You might have one of those things. You might have none. More than likely, however, your perfect attribute might be that you're perfectly average when it comes to a lot of different things.

So first things first: Stop comparing yourself to the greatest in the world. I'd forgive a lot of mistakes in a culinary student, but I would never allow them to compare their work to what's being served by Thomas Keller at the French Laundry. Second: Stop thinking of that averageness as some kind of disadvantage. There's no shame in lacking world-class talent and instead being pretty good at a few things. I should know. I wouldn't say I was blessed with any particular talent. I was just hungry, willing to learn, and ready to work. In time, I came to recognize that as my superpower. You can find the thing you're best at and work on that. In time, you might just create your own superpower, and you'll appreciate that superpower more than someone who was just born with it. Then there's no telling how much you could accomplish.

LEARN TO SIT IN DISCOMFORT

Take note of what you see when you bottom out—
there's good stuff down there

As we approach the end of this book, I want to share with you one of my favorite quotes, this one courtesy of French philosopher Blaise Pascal.

"All of humanity's problems stem from man's inability to sit quietly in a room alone."

Pascal's statement about sitting quietly is an interesting choice for a guy known to constantly be on the run. But I don't share the quote here to encourage you to achieve Zen status before beginning a project. I'm sharing it because the quote speaks to me about being able to tolerate not just setbacks but dealing with the discomfort that arises when you consider the enormous gulf between the perfect vision in your head and the shabby, flawed work in progress before you. As I illustrated in the section on procrastination, too often when we have an idea, we abandon it when the initial rush of excitement fades and problems crop up. We push the discomfort away by stopping work on the idea, getting up, and going to do something else. Sure, sometimes you need a breather to refocus, but it can't be your only answer. I've found that oftentimes the best way to overcome a setback—be it rejection, an obvious flaw in your idea, or some other unforeseen obstacle—is to simply sit and, frankly, marinate in how lousy it feels.

It's strange advice, I know. But down there in the muck of having run down the wrong path or proceeded with an incomplete concept, you can usually find useful things that will help you do it right when you're ready for the next attempt or reset.

Let's say your plan for an elevated fast-food burger restaurant has hit the skids in the planning phase. You have a product that tests through the roof with rave reviews, but while you're scouting locations, you come to discover that Shake Shack is opening a franchise down the street in six months. Yeah, you love your idea, and truth be told, your personal touch on those burgers puts you in the same conversation as Shake Shack, even a little better. But opening at the exact same time against a behemoth of a corporate franchise is rightfully giving you pause. Forget about the food; your main competition is backed by virtually limitless resources. If you somehow manage to make a bigger splash in the beginning, they can weather that storm, and besides their built-in name recognition, they can promote and run specials just to hurt you. (I'm not trying to make them sound like jerks—this is just how the game is played.)

The news that Shake Shack is coming to town and bogarting your whole market would be enough to make anyone push back from the table in frustration and forget the whole idea.

But instead of doing that, let's say you sit there in that discomfort and let all the crappy feelings wash over you. The anxiety, the anger, the frustration, the overwhelming sense of powerlessness. Sit with them. Really feel them. Grieve for your idea. It deserves a moment of silence, doesn't it? You put a lot of love into this.

I really believe that only once you've felt and identified the cause of each of these emotions can you move forward with a new and better plan. Pushing the discomfort away immediately is a mistake because it deprives you of an opportunity to really deep-dive in your analysis. Had you indulged the initial impulse to whip out your phone and start manically bouncing between social media apps in search of a distraction, you wouldn't be able to feel the intense, crystallizing pain that would have allowed you to learn. To identify the finer points of your own vulnerabilities and avoid making those same mistakes in the future instead of doing what most people do, which is forget the details because they ran away from the pain, only to try something remarkably similar again in hopes that they get lucky on the redo.

This advice doesn't just go for the business world. The best creative types of all kinds—writers, artists, and actors at the very top of their fields—talk about failure and discomfort as their greatest teachers. Actors who can sit in the discomfort of watching a terrible movie they were in will always learn more than the ones who refuse to look. The same goes for writers who can read their own lousy work without flinching. (Trust me on this one; writing a book is a long journey, and not every day ended with pages that were ready for the printer.) Ditto for stand-up comedians who bomb. It takes a long time to develop the instincts to read a crowd accurately and nail down the perfect timing. And when comedians bomb, it's lonely as hell; it's just them up there and they're doing something intensely personal that the audience is rejecting. Ever work up the courage to ask someone out on a date only to have them stare back flabbergasted? Take that feeling and multiply it by a hundred, and you can begin to understand what it's like to bomb as a comedian. Or what it's like to have a full boardroom squirm in their seats and send you on your way after a pitch, or to be an actor on an audition who stayed up all night memorizing a long monologue only to be sent packing after delivering just two lines, or to pour your lifeblood into a new business and have the whole community ignore your grand opening.

I'll never sugarcoat it; it's hard out there. Damn hard. Whatever business you're trying to build. If it weren't so damn hard, everyone would be doing it. There's no way to make it easier—all you can do is get thicker skin. You get thicker skin, of course, by allowing calluses to build up, and you can only get those by enduring discomfort.

Here we come back to the age-old question of how many times you should be expected to fail before finally meeting with victory. It's also where the rise-and-grind crowd, the ubiquitous purveyors of grit and always-sunny never-give-up-on-your-dreams platitudes is met with a lot of criticism.

Well, not everyone should keep following their dreams, critics will say. *They've got bills to pay and they'll never be able to if they keep chasing fame and fortune.*

That's a valid concern. Some people who yearn and reach and strive for years or decades or their whole lives just never make it. If you've been chasing a big dream, the thought of eventually going to your grave without ever seeing the promised land can be too much to bear. Talk about discomfort; this very notion is the first thing we push away.

Yet again, I say sit there in that discomfort. Think hard about what it would mean to chase your dream to the very end of your life and only know the feeling of having come up short. I've thought about it as it pertains to my own dreams and goals, and as much as it initially turned my stomach to think about never making it there, I ultimately decided to keep going. Why? Because the thought of leaving this world and having left some effort on the table turned my stomach even more.

But that was *my* decision. It's how I felt about my prospects, my confidence in my own abilities, and how I wanted to spend my time on this Earth. I can't make the decision for you. All I can tell you is to sit in the discomfort and think hard.

Are you OK with leaving something on the table? Or do you demand more of yourself? What is the life that is more worth living? I cast no judgment on whatever decision you come to. Not that it should matter at this point. Your opinion on this is the only one that matters. Your decision to hang on and try for another six months or a year or five or ten must be yours and yours alone.

But if you've had the guts to really try—to put yourself out there, take risks, and work your tail off—I want you to know that I'm proud of you. Truly. I know what it takes and why so many people opt for the conventional even when they go to bed every night dreaming of so much more. If you gave it your best, you're already a winner in my book. It's my sincerest hope that you can give yourself the same credit.

THE VALUE OF HATERS

How your adversaries can become your greatest teachers

In parting, I want you to know that everything I have shared with you about how to mentally approach the business world— how to think and behave like a leader, foresee obstacles before they become serious issues, do the appropriate digging to make the right hires, and do all your homework before your big prod- uct launch—it won't be enough. Though you've likely gotten your head around that particular stubborn fact already. Books, classes, seminars—all these resources can be great. Personally, I've found that more than the specific information they provide, reading more books on the topic I'm interested in keeps my mind stimulated and focused on the task I want to complete. Especially if what you want to do next isn't directly related to what you do now, voraciously reading or consuming podcasts or YouTube videos on the new subject can be a great way to redi- rect your brainpower to, in effect, normalize thinking about your big plans all day long. That's a cumulative effect, and its power is greater than any one piece of media can provide. I hope you've gotten both things from this book: specific infor- mation to take under advisement, and another piece of inspira- tion that you can use as a springboard going forward.

Not surprisingly, there are certain lessons that can't be learned in any book. To extract these lessons, they simply must be experienced. For starters, let's take Malcolm Gladwell's 10,000-hours-to-mastery rule, as I happen to think this is as good a guide as any. If this rule is true, you already know that no one else can put in those hours of practice for you. Think about that: whether you give yourself three weeks of vacation per year or not (and few entrepreneurs starting out have the patience or the luxury of doing that), the 10,000 hours breaks down into about five years of work, assuming a 40-hour workweek during that time (again, almost every business owner puts in more, but I find it helpful to throw the 10,000 hours up against the most relatable benchmark).

For aspiring restaurateurs, that would be five years of practice until you're experienced enough to run the kitchen; it's another five years of business experience and study until you've got enough know-how to effectively run the whole establishment. Take those years as a percentage of the average life expectancy, and, well, to call it daunting is an understatement. Our time on this Earth is short and precious, and the feeling of having wasted any of it on an endeavor that didn't yield the intended result is a heavy one to live with.

Again, you must weigh that risk against the potential regret of having never given it your all and decide for yourself which path you must take. If you think it all the way through, weighing every pro and con, and then decide to step away, I applaud your wisdom and wish you nothing but the best, wherever the road takes you from here. I further urge you to refuse to carry any of the phony societal guilt you've been encouraged to carry because you "gave up on your dream." Nonsense. You thought it through and you chose something else for yourself. When I say that the entrepreneurial life isn't for everyone, I don't say it to put myself on a pedestal and look down on others who chose not to follow.

Yes, well, some of us have the moxie and some don't. Pity you couldn't join me up here . . .

Looks funny written out like that, but there's a lot of this sentiment going around. Do yourself a favor and unfollow any social media accounts that spout nonsense like this. The really funny thing about most of the entrepreneurial influencers is that very few of them ever created any products of their own; the only business they ever built was the one they have now, wherein they "coach" unsuspecting rubes.

Now, for the folks who are still all in on those big crazy dreams, who've weighed the risks and embraced them all, I have one last piece of advice for you, and it concerns haters.

Not everyone in your life is going to be happy about what you're doing. They're going to behave like imbeciles. If your new venture goes poorly, they'll be the first to shake their heads and say, "See? Told you it was a bad idea." If it goes well, they'll treat you differently, insisting it's you who forgot your roots and the "little people." They'll look for every little shift in your behavior to fling a "You've changed" in your direction, and they will absolutely be using it as a pejorative. Meanwhile, of course success is going to change you. It's going to put more money in your pocket and you're not going to be so stressed all the time about your expenses. It's going to open you up to tons of new people, new ideas, and new experiences. In the best-case scenario, it's going to make you *happy*.

So here's what I want you to do when you encounter one of these haters: Don't cut them off. Pull them in. Listen to everything they say about why it's a bad idea and a bad time, why you're not ready now and maybe never will be, how the people who've made it are all special, and you, well, you're just you, and you'll never be one of them.

An ambitious goal is a rocket ship that requires many diverse fuel sources. I've been happy to provide you with the knowledge I've acquired through my experience and to act as your coach and biggest fan. You'll need people like me, but trust me: you'll also need haters, because they can provide one final, crucial lesson that all the people who are rooting for you can never give you. That's because haters will teach you how bad you really want to make it. Their insecurity and piss-poor outlook on their own lives will find an easy target in a person like you with lofty ideas. They'll jump on every opportunity to poke holes in those ideas because down in the dumps where they live it can get lonely and they don't want you leaving. They need you to stay right where you are.

Only once you've met enough haters who tell you you'll never do what you want to do—and learned to rebound from all those encounters without losing enthusiasm—can you be truly ready. Don't worry about going out and finding haters or worrying if you'll ever encounter enough. They are legion and they are *everywhere*. I still meet them all the time, and guess what they tell me about the next things I have planned for my life and career? They tell me I can't do it. Because I've enjoyed a bit of success— and I'm kind of a big dude—they're a little less brazen about directly insulting me, but they're still out here and they still chirp. I've learned to love them for all the fuel they don't even know they're providing.

Some would call it petty, having such a long memory or "keeping a list" of these folks. It's nothing of the sort. They're inadvertent helpers, and I mean it when I say be thankful for them. Besides, I don't believe in keeping grudges. All of them are welcome to stand in line to get into your grand opening, your product launch, or whatever your big moment looks like. And they'll elbow other customers in line, point you out, and say, "Hey, you know, we go way back."

Sure we do, buddy. And your money's just as good as anyone else's, so pay up.

ACKNOWLEDGMENTS

First and foremost, I wish to thank my family for being with me on every step of this crazy journey. Thank you to my wife, Gail, my best friend, the love of my life, and my rock. To my daughters, Annalise and Talia, who make me prouder than I can ever properly express; I am so grateful that I get to be your dad. To my mom, Pat: I told you I'd wind up doing something really cool. Thanks for responding, "I know."

This book wasn't just a labor of love, but a team effort in the truest sense. Every member of Team Irvine contributed in some fashion, whether it was articulating specific lessons that could be instructive to aspiring entrepreneurs, submitting general commentary, or proofreading the earliest drafts. I am incredibly lucky to get to work with such a dynamic group of people who inspire me to bring my best every day.

Thanks especially to . . .

My chief operating officer, Justin Leonard. So much of the success of Team Irvine is due to Justin's uncanny ability to juggle so many disparate projects at once. His knowledge and wisdom in so many areas of the business and entertainment worlds as well as his deft negotiating skills make him an indispensable partner.

My VP of finance, Joshua Lingenfelter, whose "high-performance accounting" I extolled here in these pages. His extensive knowledge of business writing helped guide me toward territory that hadn't been as thoroughly explored in other business books and to which I could add a personal touch.

Ryan Coyne, who goes above and beyond the call every day and keeps these companies running in so many different ways. Thank you.

My chefs: Shane Cash, Darryl Moiles, Brian Goodman, and Tito Marino. As I wrote in this book, I wouldn't be keen to go head-to-head in a cooking competition with any of you. I'm grateful every day to have you in the trenches with me and for the wisdom you shared to help me write this. The best boss-employee relationships are the mutually beneficial ones, and you challenge me to go further every day with your work ethic and creativity.

Restaurant: Impossible executive producer Jill Littman; your hard work and diligence in crafting TV that people still find compelling after all these years created the conditions that would put me in the way of so many of the people and lessons that allowed me to write this book. You and your team's research for the *Restaurant: Impossible* case studies was incredible. And, well, you're just an all-around badass.

Restaurant: Impossible builder Tom Bury and designers Lynn Kegan and Taniya Nayak; I'm no fool and I know I can't do it all. For over three hundred episodes, you have not only applied your boundless creativity and ingenuity to remodel restaurants for people who needed it so badly; you've been a steadying force for me—a calm in the eye of the storm. While I'm racking my brain to figure out a way to get my point across to the failing owners, you work through the night with unnatural calm, transforming eyesores into beautiful new restaurants. We couldn't do this show without you, and I'm eternally grateful for you and your crews.

Robert Irvine Foods president, Gary Shives. Since you're the quintessential example of the honest and honorable salesman, I rest easy knowing that you're the one out there interfacing with the customers and representing me to the rest of the world.

The Robert Irvine Foundation team, especially core members Judy Otter, Dave Reid, Anthony Spadaro, and board members Pam Swan, Scott Sonnemaker, and David Jeffries. My passion for giving back to our nation's veterans and first responders is the thing that makes all this hard work so worthwhile, and collectively you form the engine that makes it all possible. To Dave Reid: Your sacrifice on behalf of this nation is something that inspired me from the day I met you and continues to motivate me every day. We do what we do for the men and women just like you.

The FitCrunch team, especially Patrick Cornacchiulo, Dave Plowden, Elena Fusaro, Mike Spinosa, and Taylor Piazza. About a decade ago, I remember sharing the first FitCrunch prototype bars with friends and family and seeing the smiles on their faces as it dawned on them that a healthy snack could taste this good. Since then, you've helped spread those smiles to more corners of this world than I imagined possible and turned the brand into a true juggernaut. You're professionals through and through, and you prove to me time and again that nothing is impossible.

The Boardroom/Irvine Spirits team, especially co-owners Marat Mamedov, Zsuzsa Palotas, and Vlad Mamedov. I'm nothing but lucky that a chance meeting led to our partnership and the continued growth of this company. Irvine's gin and vodka are poised to take over the world, and when they do, it will be your hard work and vision that made it possible.

To the entire HarperCollins team for their thoughtful feedback throughout this process, especially editor Tim Burgard, who immediately recognized the strengths in the first draft and provided so many creative ideas to make it even stronger.

To the small business owners and salespeople who provided insight into so many diverse areas of the business world, this book is better because of your input. These include Gordana Biernat, Asa Briggs, Joshua Darbee, Michael Donnelly, Mike Geremia, Leah Jantzen, James Johnson, Erin Kraus, Kendra McCarrick Beavis, Ryan Megenedy, Ed "Pops" Meier, A. Chip Muller, Stephen Plunkett, Heather Quinlan, John Quinlan, Brent Stig-Kraus, Tommy Tsiatsis, and Michael Tuthill.

To the beta readers—Maria Tuthill Murphy, Jill Tuthill, and Christopher Tuthill—thank you for dutifully hunting for typos and for the earliest rave reviews. You have excellent taste, so your approval is worth quite a lot to me.

Last, to you, the reader: Thank you for trying to make something great. Whether you will ultimately meet your own definition of success is up to you. But I truly believe in my heart of hearts that this world is made better and richer just by your trying. We may not always get to see our grandest plans come to fruition, but a genuine effort in a worthy cause has its own value. Always remember: you never know who you're inspiring with that effort. As you go out there and fight the good fight, know that I see you.

INDEX

A

accountability, 19–23
accounting, high-performance, 67–68
anger issues, 46–47, 110–111. *See also* harassment
announcements, public, 146–149
attitude shifts, 23
authentic voice, 81–86
averageness, 200

B

Beats 'N Eats, 80
Benton, Kerry, 110–113
Biernat, Gordana, 87–88, 92
Boardroom Spirits, 54–55
Brown, Brené, 85–86
Brunet, Robert "Chef BB," 157–160

C

Café No Fur (Las Vegas), 21–23
Cash, Shane, 117, 137
Chan, Kevin, 22–23
change
    commitment to, 98–102
    as constant, 93–95
    military, technological change in, 95–97

clichés, 160–166, 197
coaching, 121–122
comfort zones, 94–95
consumer education, 138–139
core competency, 47, 48
coronavirus pandemic, 53–55, 172, 188
corporate size, 15
cost-benefit analysis, 68
Country Cow/Covered Bridge Farm Table (Campton, NY), 110–113
crisis, leading through, 53–60
cruft, 195–196
crunch-time cycle, 172
Currence, Deborah, 122
Curry, Steph, 187–188
cybersecurity, 57

D

data
    as hard facts, 59
    securing, 57
    selling with, 65–69
delegating, 5–6, 194–196
Deraney, Christopher, 13–15
Deraney's Two City Tavern (Barnesville, GA), 13–15
Dinner: Impossible, 63

discomfort, sitting in, 200–204
Disney, Walt, 179–181
disorganization, 35–37
diversification vs. specialization, 163–164

E
education, lifelong, 167–170
ego
   case study, 157–160
   conflicting, 39, 40
   as core issue, 151–154
   harassment and, 28–32
   hiring and, 117
   luck and, 156–157
   self-reflection and, 154–156
emotional intelligence, 24–32
employees. *See also* hiring
   accountability and, 19–23
   emotional intelligence and, 24–32
   ideas from, 8
   investing in, 15–18
   kiss-up-and-kick-down types, 30–31
   leading by example, 10–15
   "losing" good people, 17
   low-level, communicating with, 30–31
   micromanaging, 3–9, 47
   motivation and, 16
   setting expectations, 12
   staying engaged with, during crisis, 57
   training of, 41–42, 168
   trusting, 7–9
example, leading by, 10–12
exercise, 173–174
expectations, setting, 12

F
failure
   blame and, 21
   as driver, 182
   flat chicken initiative, 137–139
   of great ideas, 115
   "it's who you know" and, 197
   leaving room for, 139
   reframing, 178
   sitting with, 202
   sunk cost fallacy and, 113
   your "why" and, 127
family financing, 113–116
family negativity and risk aversion, 182–183
fear, 175–176
Felter, George, 46–48
Ferriss, Tim, 175
financing. *See* money
finding what you're best at, 132–137
firing, 9
FitCrunch, 54
Fresh Kitchen by Robert Irvine, 19–20, 100, 117
From Across the Pond (Colleyville, TX), 130–132

G
giving back, 118–123
Gladwell, Malcolm, 205
"go big or go home," 162–163
Gonzales, Yhessa, 22–23
Goodman, Brian, 116
gratitude, 172–173
Green, Ninkia, 143–145
Grille No. 13 (Waldorf, MD), 194–196
growth. *See* scale and growth

H
harassment, 28–32, 141–142. *See also* anger issues
hardship, 181–182
haters, value of, 205–208
"having it all," 192–193

Herdman, Dan, 131–132
Hill, Napoleon, 6
hiring
  ego and, 117
  key hires, 116–118
  time outside the interview,
    11–12
  trust and, 8–9
honesty, in sales, 69–70
humility, 168–169

I

ideas
  ego and, 152–154
  from employees, 8
  exercise and, 173–174
  failure of great ideas, 115
  haters and, 208
  procrastination and, 175–178
"it's not who you are, it's who you
  know," 197–200

J

Jefferson, Calvin, 143–145
Jeffries, David, 108, 115–116
Joe Willy's Fish Shack/Seafood
  House (Fishkill, NY), 3–7

K

Kamen, Dean, 105
Kegan, Lynn, 22–23
kiss-up-and-kick-down types,
  30–31

L

leadership
  crisis and, 53–60
  ego and, 40
  leading by example and pitching
    in, 10–15
  trust and, 7–9
learning, lifelong, 167–170

Leonard, Justin, 27–30, 75, 140
Leonzi, Jenny, 110–113
"let's pivot to . . . ," 166
Lingenfelter, Josh, 67–68
Littlejohn, Cheryl, 120–123
Littman, Jill, 141
luck, 156–157

M

Mandino, Og, 54
Marino, Tito, 116
meetings, exploratory, 75–78
the micro and the macro, 171–173
micromanagement, 3–8, 47, 122
military, technological change in,
  95–97
mise en place ("everything in its
  place"), 33–37
mistakes, owning, 19–21
Moiles, Darryl, 116–117
Momma Pearl's Cajun Kitchen
  (Colorado Springs), 157–160
money
  case study, 120–123
  family financing, 113–116
  giving back, 118–123
  as means to an end, 180
  relationship stress and,
    109–113
  school of "money is everything"
    vs. school of altruism,
    107–108
Mr. B's Restaurant (Tampa, FL),
  143–145
"my door is always open," 164–165

N

nCino, 93–94
negativity, 183–184
"no risk, no reward," 163–164
"no," saying, 70–72
nostalgia, 102–103

O

open-door policy, 164–165
opening a restaurant, 49–50, 116
Oprah, 81–82

P

panic, 55
Park Vue Soul Food Bar &
    Restaurant (Buffalo), 35–37
Parresol, Eric, Jodi, and Melissa,
    135–136
partnerships
    downsides and upsides, 182
    end of, 72–74
    meetings and, 75
    relationship stress and, 109–113
    Twitter and, 79–80
Pascal, Blaise, 200–201
passion, 128–130
Paul's Bowling (Paterson, NJ), 97–98
persistence, 179–186
Person, Michael, 184–186
philanthropy, 118–123
Pierce, Katie, 194–196
"pivot," 166
A Pizza Melody (Las Vegas), 46–48
preparation
    case studies, 35–37, 46–48
    for crises, 53–60
    going big and mistakes, 37–40
    mise en place ("everything in its
        place"), 33–37
    opening a restaurant, 49–50
    recipes, scalability of, 43–45
    shortcuts as fatal, 51–52
    training as, 41–42
procrastination, 175–178
public announcements, 146–149

R

rejection, 62
relationship stress, 109–113

Restaurant: Impossible
    authentic voice and, 82–83
    ego as core issue, 151–154
    hardship and, 181
    key hires for, 116–117
    passion and, 129
    pitching, 63
    return of, 103–104
    romantic partners on, 108–109
    technology in, 97–98, 103–104
Restaurant: Impossible case studies
    From Across the Pond, 130–132
    Café No Fur, 21–23
    Country Cow/Covered Bridge
        Farm Table, 110–113
    Deraney's Two City Tavern,
        13–15
    Grille No. 13, 194–196
    Joe Willy's Fish Shack/Seafood
        House, 3–7
    Momma Pearl's Cajun Kitchen,
        157–160
    Mr. B's Restaurant, 143–145
    Park Vue Soul Food Bar &
        Restaurant, 35–37
    Paul's Bowling, 97–98
    A Pizza Melody, 46–48
    The Ship Inn, 184–186
    Smith's Soul Food Bistro,
        120–123
    Turnpike's Rest Stop, 134–137
risk mitigation
    aversion to risk, 182–183
    mise en place and, 34–35
    "no risk, no reward" vs.,
        163–164
Robert Irvine Foods
    change and, 99–100
    flat chicken failure, 137–139
    key hire, 117
    partnerships and, 72–74
    salesmanship and, 67–68

Robert Irvine Foundation
    giving back, 118–119
    grants, 54, 58
    passion and, 129
    proceeds going to, 83
    social media and, 80
Robert Irvine's Eat!, 116
Robert Irvine's Public House, 100,
    116–117

S
sales
    data and, 65–69
    ending a partnership, 72–74
    honesty in, 69–70
    meetings, exploratory, 75–78
    the power vested in yourself,
        61–65
    rejection, 62
    saying no and being choosy,
        70–72
    you are always selling, 64–65
scale and growth
    going big, 37–41
    scaling up, 43–48
    steady, sustained growth,
        162–163, 187–188
Schlitter, Terry, 46–48
Schwarzenegger, Arnold, 183
self-awareness, 139–145
self-reflection, 102–105, 154–155
Sellers, Jodie, 131
The Ship Inn (Exton, PA), 184–186
Shives, Gary, 73
shortcuts, 51–52, 122–123
Smith's Soul Food Bistro (Gastonia,
    NC), 120–123
social media
    authentic voice and being real,
        81–86
    big announcements, danger in,
        146–149

holding back or saying nothing,
        88–92
    positivity and, 86–88
    power of, 79–80
    procrastination and, 177, 178
    staying engaged with customers,
        56
stubbornness, 4–5, 10, 74, 97, 152
students for life, 167–170
success. *See also Restaurant:*
    Impossible case studies
    accepting reality and, 199–200
    best practices, 55–60
    big-picture view and, 74
    Walt Disney and, 179–180
    ego and, 155–156
    expectations of employees and,
        12
    experience, instincts, and tastes
        and, 45
    "having it all," 192–193
    as jagged path, 116, 117
    as ongoing journey, 167–168
    personal popularity and, 82
    publicly announcing, 130,
        146–149
    rejection and, 62
    what you're best at and, 134
    your "why" and, 127, 128
sunk cost fallacy, 112–113

T
teaching, 168
technology
    change as constant, 93–95
    commitment to change, 98–102
    military, technological change in,
        95–97
    in *Restaurant: Impossible*, 97–98,
        103–104
    self-reflection and, 102–105
"think outside the box," 161

training, 41–42, 168
trendiness, 132–137
trust
  honesty and, 70
  leadership style and, 7–9
  micromanaging and, 4
Turnpike's Rest Stop (Springfield,
  FL), 134–137
Twitter, 79–80, 85, 86. *See also*
  social media

V
value, adding, 54
voice, authentic, 81–86

W
West, Harrita, 35–36
White, Joe, 3–7
"why," 127–130
Williams, Schenita, 35–36

winning the day
  even-keeled, long-term
    approach, 187–188
  the macro and the micro,
    171–173
  persistence, 179–186
  procrastination, 175–178
  small habits to win each day,
    172–175
work-life balance
  case study, 194–196
  discomfort, sitting in, 200–204
  hard work, 189–192
  haters, value of, 205–208
  "it's not who you are, it's who
    you know," 197–200
  trade-offs, 192–194

Y
Yelp, 102

ABOUT THE AUTHORS

ROBERT IRVINE

Robert Irvine is a world-class chef and entrepreneur, and a tireless philanthropic supporter of our nation's military. The host of Food Network's hit show *Restaurant: Impossible*, he has given struggling restaurateurs a second chance to turn their lives and businesses around in more than three hundred episodes and counting.

He would know a thing or two about running a successful business. In addition to his restaurants—Robert Irvine's Public House at the Tropicana in Las Vegas and Fresh Kitchen by Robert Irvine within the Pentagon—he is the owner of Fit-Crunch, whose protein bars, powders, and snacks are available nationwide; Robert Irvine Foods, which makes prepared, restaurant-quality dishes available in grocery stores; and the Lansdale, Pennsylvania–based Boardroom Spirits, creators of handcrafted whiskey, rum, and flagship products Irvine's Precision Distilled Vodka and Irvine's American Dry Gin.

A portion of the proceeds from all of Robert's endeavors benefit the Robert Irvine Foundation. Created in 2014, the foundation gives back to our servicemen and -women and first responders. Funds raised help at-need veterans and first responders in a variety of ways: training service dogs, making mental health and wellness services available to veterans in need, providing mobility devices for the disabled, and much more.

For his charitable work and service on numerous USO tours, Robert is the recipient of several civilian honors, including Honorary Chief Petty Officer of the United States Navy and the Medal of Honor Society's Bob Hope Award.

When not filming for television or working overseas with the USO, he can be found on tour with *Robert Irvine LIVE*, an unpredictable interactive cooking challenge done before a live audience in packed theaters.

He is the distinguished author of four previous books: *Mission: Cook!*, *Impossible to Easy*, *Fit Fuel*, and *Family Table by Robert Irvine*.

He lives in Tampa, Florida, with his wife, Gail Kim-Irvine.

Learn more at chefirvine.com.

MATT TUTHILL

A journalist with more than twenty years of experience, Matt Tuthill serves as vice president of content and communications for Robert Irvine. The coauthor of *Fit Fuel* and *Family Table by Robert Irvine*, he also runs *Robert Irvine Magazine*, a digital publication delivering recipes, workouts, and motivational content (RobertIrvineMagazine.com). He lives on Long Island with his wife, Jill, and their two sons, Quinn Angelo and Axel Shawn. Learn more at matt-tuthill.com.